The Show Must NOT Go On

We would be pleased to keep you on our mailing list for new catalogues. Please send your name and address to :

**Robert Davies Publishing, P.O. Box 702,
Outremont, QC H2V 4N6**

Senator Royce Frith and Len Kuchar

The Show Must NOT Go On

ROBERT DAVIES PUBLISHING
MONTREAL–TORONTO

DISTRIBUTED IN CANADA BY

Stewart House
481 University Avenue, Suite 900
Toronto, Ontario M5G 2E9

☎ (Ontario & Quebec) 1-800-268-5707
☎ (rest of Canada) 1-800-268-5742

ISBN 1-895854-21-0
Copyright © 1993,
Robert Davies Publishing, a division of l'Étincelle éditeur.
1   2   3   93   94

*The authors acknowledge
the indispensible collaboration
of Renée Graf in the
production of this book.*

Table of Contents

Introduction 9

Chapter 1 — The Reluctant Bride 13

Chapter 2 — The Conservative Candidate with Compassion 16

Chapter 3 — "Jobs, Jobs, Jobs" and "Sacred Trusts" on the Road to Parliament 28

Chapter 4 — The "Honorable" Member from Central Nova 36

Chapter 5 — "You had an Option" - Election '84 52

Chapter 6 — Now that we're elected, how do we keep our promises, particularly on R&D 66

Chapter 7 — The One Trillion Dollar Man 77

Chapter 8 — Constitutional Revisionism 93

Chapter 9 — Patronage from "the Pinocchio of Politics" 105

Chapter 10 — "Honest" Brian v. "Traitor" John - Election '88 127

Chapter 11 — "Forget there was an election" and everything we said 137

Chapter 12 — Meanwhile... 148

Chapter 13 — "A New Standard of Morality" 164

Conclusion — O'Canada 181

INTRODUCTION

JUNE 11, 1993; THE OTTAWA CIVIC CENTRE. Prime Minister Brian Mulroney delivers his swan-song to Tory delegates gathered to choose his successor. His parting words:

"We kept our word."

It might take a search warrant to find many Canadians who remember it that way.

But while most Canadians are sure that Mr. Mulroney's statement is false — outlandishly so — how many can remember why? The Goebbels technique still works: if you are going to lie, make it such a whopper, so breathtakingly false, that you stun your audience out of the known truth.

So the truth being that Mr. Mulroney did not keep his word, that he made promises for only one purpose — to win elections — and having won in '84, began eight years of an administration which dragged behind it a long train of broken promises. That train eventually became so heavy and obvious to all Canadians that it dragged Mr. Mulroney under and forced his resignation. If he had kept his word, he might now be seeking a third mandate from Canadians. Instead he appears to pull his successor down with him.

The Conservative administration is at a record-breaking low in popularity, probably largely because of its disgraceful record and solid reputation for breaking promises and ignoring the welfare of most Canadians in favor of the welfare of its wealthy corporate supporters.

It has been said that an unpopular or even disgraced government's best friend is the people's short memory. This book is a stroll down the memory lane of this Conservative government's nine years of unfulfilled promise, broken promises and cruel cynicism. Here we go.

First, a setting and some propositions to start us off. Following his 1983 by-election victory in Central Nova, soon-to-be Prime

THE SHOW MUST NOT GO ON

Minister Brian Mulroney was asked by Richard Gwyn how he would like to be remembered if given a chance to govern the country. Mr. Mulroney replied:

> **There are two priorities I would hope to be remembered for if I am given the opportunity. The first would be to achieve a new kind of prosperity, an enduring prosperity....**
>
> **My second goal would be to restore in Canada a society of which the hallmark would be tolerance.** (*Toronto Star*, Aug. 31/83)

It is tempting to limit our attention to Mr. Mulroney's own goals, to ask whether Canada is now blessed with a tolerant society and a new prosperity. That, however, would be too easy, and perhaps unfair because the question is not simply whether Prime Minister Mulroney met his own expectations, but whether he met the expectations he planted and then nurtured in Canadians.

Another important test is how the Mulroney record compares to that of previous governments and how it measures up to commonly-held principles of good government.

Against both, the grade must be an F, for failure.

Taking Mr. Mulroney's own objectives, we see not tolerance, but growing intolerance and cleavages in society. Instead of a new prosperity, we are, in the words of the Canadian Chamber of Commerce, **"in the midst of a national fiscal crisis, and on the precipice of a national economic crisis."** (*Financial Post*, April 20/93)

Taking what was promised to Canadians, we would simply have to allege fraud. If general elections were contracts, the courts would have ordered rescission long ago on the ground of fraudulent misrepresentation. Promises were broken constantly, incessantly, unremittingly. There then followed more promises, which suffered the same fate. Nothing short of olympic-class promise-breaking.

Against a standard of generally recognized principles of good government, and the record of previous administrations, the Mulroney years were not years of good government. Canadians are now aware of just how bad this administration was for everyone;

INTRODUCTION

everyone, that is, except the government's coterie of privileged friends.

We believe that historians will join the Mulroney years to the R.B. Bennett years, as a period of broken trust and lost hope. A new generation of Canadians has learned the truth of the words of their grandparents: *"Tory times are hard times."* In 1983, however, this new generation joined other Canadians in high expectations of candidate Mulroney when he stepped forward into the public spotlight.

And speaking of history — the judgments of historians will come forth in due course. Our quick look at the record - nine years of promise vs. performance - is simply to help those who want to refresh their memories about what was said vs. what was done during those nine years. We are not trying to retell the GST and Free Trade stories — they have been well documented. But in those nine years, there was much more not so well documented and therefore not so well remembered.

A good place to begin is Winnipeg, January 31, 1983.

1.

THE RELUCTANT BRIDE

THE SCENE IS THE OFFICE OF THE MANAGER of the Winnipeg Convention Centre. The players are Joe Clark and his wife Maureen McTeer, David MacDonald and his wife Sandra, Finlay MacDonald, Peter Harder, Jake Epp, Marcel Danis, Tony Saunders, Terry Yates, and Lowell Murray. An employee of the accounting firm Touche Ross and Partners enters the room. He hands Mr. Clark an envelope.

> Clark loosened the seal of the envelope and took out the paper inside. "Well...," said Clark, his voice barely audible, his eyes still staring at the page. Slowly he raised his head and spoke so everyone could hear: "66.9." Everyone in the room gasped. Clark's gaze met Lowell Murray's. Murray let out his breath, lowered his eyes and shook his head. "It's not enough," was all he said. (*Contenders: The Tory Quest for Power* - Martin, Gregg and Perlin — p. 4)

Finlay MacDonald suggested: "I don't think we should do anything hasty," but Clark chose to heed Senator Murray's advice. He called for a leadership convention.

Though this announcement marked the beginning of the end for Mr. Clark as party leader, apparently it had no ill effect on Clark's chief strategist, Senator Lowell Murray, who went on to become the Government Leader in the Senate at the request of Mr. Clark's successor. More recently, he has become Prime Minister Kim Campbell's confidant and her choice as Senate Government Leader.

But what of Mr. Clark's immediate successor? What was his reaction? Well, if his words are to be believed, Mr. Mulroney had very little interest in what was happening. He would not even say whether he was interested in being a leadership candidate.

THE RELUCTANT BRIDE

"Running for the PC leadership is 'the last thing' on his mind, the Iron Ore Co. of Canada president told a Gazette reporter who tracked him down...." (*Montreal Gazette*, Feb. 5/83)

A week later, reporters caught up with Mr. Mulroney in Schefferville, Quebec. When questioned about his political ambitions, Mr. Mulroney replied:

"I don't want to appear coy, but my job here is to run the company. Politics are my recreation." (*Globe and Mail*, Feb. 12/83)

But Mr. Mulroney was in Schefferville not to run his company, but to explain why his company was running out of town. As for politics being his recreation — most Canadians, probably including Mr. Clark, can now only dream of it having remained just that.

And, the bride continued to be reluctant. When 2000 copies of a letter extolling the virtues of a certain unnamed **"charismatic Quebec businessman"** were sent to potential Quebec delegates, Mr. Mulroney professed ignorance, though the letter was signed by Jean Bazin, Keith Morgan and Rodrigue Pageau, his top Quebec organizers. While in Newfoundland, Mr. Mulroney claimed he had not found time even to think about running. **"But when a leadership convention is called - presumably this weekend - I will then, of course, begin to take a look at it."** (*Montreal Gazette*, Feb. 16/83)

The following month, there was a "spontaneous" rally at the Queen Elizabeth Hotel in Montreal, where two or three thousand supporters gathered to reassure the reluctant bride.

Mr. Mulroney's reluctance to declare was puzzling considering the single-minded way he had worked to undermine Mr. Clark's leadership. His manoeuvrings against Clark are well documented. Less well-known is the personal disdain he had for the leader of his party. When a journalist remarked that Mr. Clark still enjoyed wide-spread support within the party, Mulroney replied:

"It's sad when a guy mistakes sympathy for support. He's like a dinner guest who won't leave your house after the

—14—

meal is over. You get him up from the table and aim him towards the open door but he clings to the door with his fingertips." (*Montreal Gazette,* March 19/83)

Pause, and quick fast-forward to spring 1993 when after a long struggle Mr. Mulroney's own fingertips were pried from the doorway - and in the absence of any sympathy that could be mistaken for support. But back to early in 1983, when he couldn't persuade those same fingers to throw his hat into the ring. Mulroney explained he was hesitating because he first wanted to ensure that **"serious Conservatives"** and the people at the grass roots believed he had **"a contribution to make."** There was also an additional consideration.

"As you know," he said, "I'm not a rich man. I have three young children, so it's a big decision which must be weighed very carefully." (*Montreal Gazette,* March 12/83)

That statement from the President of the Iron Ore Company of Canada is certainly a curiosity, and becomes "curiouser and curiouser," as Alice would say, the more one thinks about it. In view of his lifestyle before and after retirement, one can only say that he has made great strides in the intervening period. And his being "not a rich man" did not seem to help him empathize with less fortunate Canadians, in spite of his talk;

"I am a caring, compassionate Conservative on all social matters, who understands that government has a major role to play in looking after the disadvantaged and the dispossessed." (*Globe and Mail,* March 15/83)

On March 21, 1983, that "compassionate Conservative" finally announced that he would be a candidate for the leadership of the federal party with the appropriately oxymoronic name - the Progressive Conservative Party. It was to be a perfect fit. For Canadians, it would prove to be a different story.

2.

THE CONSERVATIVE CANDIDATE WITH COMPASSION

MR. MULRONEY'S CANDIDACY STARTED VERY PROMISINGLY, in several senses of the word. When Mulroney announced that he would be running for the leadership of the Conservative Party, he walked on stage disguised in a cloak of liberalism.

> "...we Conservatives must show the Canadian people that we have about us...a dimension of tenderness.
>
> Of all the challenges of government, none is more noble, no obligation more sacred. We shall be judged both as individuals and as a political party by the manner in which we care for those unable to care for themselves.
>
> This is not the United States. We have evolved over the years our own society which has always been hallmarked by a degree of compassion which should under no circumstances ever be vitiated." (*Globe and Mail*, March 22/83)

At the time, he did not dispute the fact that the compassionate society he referred to evolved under Liberal administrations. Family allowances, pensions, medicare, and unemployment insurance owed their existence to Liberal governments and Liberal Prime Ministers, and not to R.B. Bennett or John Diefenbaker.

In fairness, we must make allowances for the newcomer to politics. As he had said, it was just his "recreation." He had no record or experience and Canadians had no experience of him. So how could they know that when candidate Mulroney spoke of "compassion," "tenderness," and "sacred" obligations, those were mere words? The real Liberal structures represented by those words, he intended to loosen and then dismantle.

But we anticipate, because in 1983, we Canadians were naïve about this new, admittedly inexperienced, Conservative politician,

THE CONSERVATIVE CANDIDATE WITH COMPASSION

attired in Liberal clothing, promising to treat Canada's social programs as sacred trusts.

When not speaking of compassion, candidate Mulroney presented himself as a man of integrity and virtue. When stories circulated about certain unsavory aspects of delegate nomination meetings, candidate Mulroney professed genuine unhappiness. He said he did not like what was happening and that he had asked his organizers to conduct themselves **"the way I conduct myself in my public and private life — with intelligence, probity and honor."** (*Montreal Gazette,* March 31/83).

In addition to promising delegates and other Canadians a political party of which compassion and probity would be the hallmarks, candidate Mulroney went on and on with some details of life under a Mulroney Conservative government.

For example, special emphasis was placed on Research and Development. In fact, it became a kind of mantra for this candidate.

"Of all the civilized industrial nations in the world none spends less on research and development in science and technology than Canada, with the exception of Iceland and Ireland." (*Guardian,* **April 27/83**)

In his book *Where I Stand,* published a month before the convention, Mr. Mulroney devoted an entire chapter to research and development. On page 39, he wrote: **"we must make a firm commitment to double the public and private funds allocated to research and development before 1985."**

One week before the convention he said:

"Productivity is our most fundamental problem and it's got to be dealt with. I will make it a highest priority. And I will immediately set in motion the process for us to overcome the tremendous disadvantages we now have in the fields of research and development and science and technology by indicating to the investment community and to the people at large the importance that I attach to doubling our commitment to research and development within the next five years." (*Toronto Star,* **June 4/83**)

THE SHOW MUST NOT GO ON

Let's resist the temptation to abandon our chronology to see how these lofty statements were translated into action by the "doubling" of our R&D expenditures since 1984 because, when running for the leadership of the P.C. party, Mr. Mulroney made many other pronouncements that should not be forgotten.

According to the *Halifax Chronicle-Herald*, Mr. Mulroney called for **"steps to develop the human resources of the country, including a massive training program for people whose skills were becoming obsolete because of the switch in industrialization."** (April 27/83) This would not be the last time Canadians heard about Mulroney's "massive training program," though no one ever got a chance to see it.

According to a *Globe and Mail* editorial, Mr. Mulroney **"has developed a realistic economic policy for putting the country back on the road to revival....He has called for a national industrial strategy."** (March 22/83) Ten years later, Canadians are still waiting for that promised national industrial strategy.

According to the *Chronicle-Herald*, Mr. Mulroney talked about how the port of Halifax **"could become the transportation key to the development of the Canadian equivalent to the United States' Silicon Valley."** (April 27/83) The *Globe and Mail* of May 3, 1983, reported how he had the same vision for Charlottetown. Ten years later, both Charlottetown and Halifax are still waiting.

While in Newcastle, New Brunswick, Mr. Mulroney promised to expand Canadian Forces Base Chatham. **"He said he'd 'hand a pink slip and a pair of running shoes to any minister' who suggested otherwise"**. (*Telegraph Journal*, May 9/83) Some years later, on the evening of April 26, 1989, the Minister of National Finance announced in his Budget speech:

> "...the government will close or reduce in size 14 military bases and stations across the country." (p. 6)

Nowhere in the Budget Papers did Mr. Wilson mention that CFB Chatham was one of the bases targeted. No doubt he remembered the stern words of his Prime Minister and feared receiving a pink slip and a pair of running shoes. It was left to the Defence Minister, Bill McKnight, to announce that CFB Chatham was being shrunk, not expanded. Neither a pink slip nor running shoes were handed out.

THE CONSERVATIVE CANDIDATE WITH COMPASSION

Pink slips and running shoes were also promised to **"self-centered, boggy-brained public servants who are skilled at manipulating Cabinet ministers like marionettes. When we come in, walking softly and carrying a big stick, it's going to cause mass cardiac arrest in the Towers-of-Power of Never-Never-Land"**. (*Telegraph Journal,* May 26/83)

He had already warned:

"I'd cut everywhere and under every circumstance. I'd cut consultants, outside lawyers and accountants, advertising, public service compensation, waste, unproductive subsidies, travel, indexed pensions and fringes, capital construction programs, capital overruns and just plain bureaucratic excess." (*Toronto Star,* March 19/83)

Really?

Is that what happened?

One of Mr. Mulroney's most effective ploys as Prime Minister was convincing Canadians that the deficit was the greatest enemy of the people and that its reduction, at any cost, would deliver us into a state of public blessedness. But just as President Reagan did, Prime Minister Mulroney ballooned that deficit by giving generous tax breaks to the very rich. And again like Reagan, he launched an assault on social programs, which were primarily of benefit to the poor and middle classes. That assault was and is justified on the grounds that our social programs, and not the tax breaks given to the very rich, were the root cause of the growth in the debt.

When the achievements of this government are recorded, one will rank at the very top: shovelling money into the vaults of the rich, while convincing the middle class that their social programs were responsible for the annual deficits. A recent example of this hypocrisy was demonstrated by Ms. Campbell, when she detailed how she was open to fiddling with our universal health care system in order to combat the deficit.

But we are getting ahead of ourselves. In 1983, candidate Mulroney publicly down-played the deficit. It was not going to be attacked directly.

> About $2 billion could be cut from the federal budget to reduce Ottawa's deficit, he [Mulroney] says, but the impact would be negligible because there's a limit to how much can be cut without disrupting vital equalization programs. Instead, he says, "what's needed is no less than the restoration of the international climate of confidence in Canada." (*Montreal Gazette*, March 19/83)

A few days before the convention, Mr. Mulroney released a forecast prepared by Data Resources of Canada. The forecast, sponsored and paid for by Mulroney's campaign team, claimed that Mulroney's policies would, by 1990, reduce the unemployment rate to 5.7%, increase R&D spending to two percent of GNP and reduce the deficit to $3.1 billion. (*Toronto Sun*, June 8/83; *Globe and Mail*, June 9/83) For those making mental notes of the difference between the fantasy and the reality of the Mulroney record, the deficit in 1990 was $30.5 billion, not $3.1 billion. Was he rolling the dice even then with a decimal point?

But as we said, the deficit was not a major concern for candidate Mulroney. He worked hard at creating the impression that the economy, coming out of recession, was the real problem, and if it could be straightened out, everything else, including the deficit, would take care of itself.

But was Mr. Mulroney up to the task? After all, he possessed not a single minute of experience in government. His answer was to remind Grant Devine, who had been elected Premier of Saskatchewan the year before, of his high qualifications.

> "He had never sat in the legislature," said Mulroney, "but voters saw in him a serious businessman capable of solving problems; a man people felt could bring other important assets to cope with the current economic climate." (*Montreal Gazette*, March 12/83)

As it turned out Mr. Devine was an appropriate role model for Mr. Mulroney. Mr. Devine "coped" so well that the television program *W-5* recently devoted an entire one-hour program to the devastating economic and fiscal consequences of Devine's policies.

THE CONSERVATIVE CANDIDATE WITH COMPASSION

It concluded that Premier Devine's policies had turned Saskatchewan into a basket case.

Lack of experience did not humble Mr. Mulroney. It empowered him. This high-flying businessman, the man who shut down Schefferville, promised to work his magic on the entire country. His presence would bring prosperity:

> "Just the mere fact of my election, along with experienced and valued colleagues from the Conservative Party, would instill a magnificent degree of optimism in the country and in the international investment community." (*Ottawa Citizen*, April 4/83)

This is not to say he didn't propose some policies to get the economy moving. One of the more interesting was tax-free municipal bonds.

> **Mulroney said the proposal would create thousands of jobs and enable municipalities to proceed with costly projects which are currently delayed because of a shortage of money.... Under his scheme, a Canadian taxpayer could purchase $10,000 worth of tax-free bonds issued by his municipality and keep all of the interest. "If you received 11 per cent a year for your investment," said Mulroney, "you'd get $1,100 at the end of the first year and you wouldn't give one cent of it to the federal or provincial governments.".... He said that if he was prime minister, he would immediately order the necessary changes to the country's tax laws.** (*Montreal Gazette*, May 11/83)

"**Immediately**", he said. That we still do not have tax-free municipal bonds 10 years later should come as no surprise now that we have learned to appreciate the nuances of the Mulroney lexicon. Whether it was specific policy options he advanced, or broad strategic strokes he proposed, the outcome was always the same, namely, the opposite of what was promised. A good example was candidate Mulroney's firm and principled stand on free trade.

Though Mr. Mulroney stressed the importance of foreign investment for our economy and a determination to forge closer relations with the United States, in 1983 he left no doubt that he understood the tightrope Canada had been walking since 1867.

> **Le candidat à la direction du Parti conservateur Brian Mulroney considère que «d'ouvrir toutes grandes les portes» du Canada au commerce américain constituerait une menace pour sa souveraineté économique et politique. ... Comparant ensuite notre voisin américain à un éléphant, M. Mulroney estime qu'il «est extrêmement dangereux de coucher avec une telle bête qui peut, durant la nuit, changer de côté, au risque et péril de son partenaire».** *(Le Devoir,* May 16/83)

He even ridiculed his pro-free trade opponent, John Crosbie:

> **He scoffed at the idea of free trade with the U.S. "It's like sleeping with an elephant - everything is fine until the elephant rolls over." Mulroney said he thought the free trade issue had been settled by the general election of 1911. "It affects our sovereignty and we are not going to have any of it."** *(Toronto Sun,* June 3/83)

This was a message he repeated constantly during his campaign to win the leadership of the Conservative party.

> **"This country could not survive with a policy of unfettered free trade. ...This is a separate country. We'd be swamped. We have in many ways a branch-plant economy, in many ways, in certain important sectors. All that would happen with that kind of concept would be the boys cranking up their plants throughout the United States in bad times and shutting their entire branch plants in Canada. It's bad enough as it is. ..."** *(Globe and Mail,* June 1/83)

At the time he probably did not know how right he was, but in 1983 he <u>was</u> right. For once, he was right. He warned that in bad times, manufacturing plants would shut down in Canada, shifting their production to the United States. That is precisely what happened. The Mulroney government brought us free trade, then a "made in Canada" recession, and the result was just as he predicted

THE CONSERVATIVE CANDIDATE WITH COMPASSION

— the loss of hundreds of thousands of manufacturing jobs. Many corporations didn't even wait for the recession to move south.

So why, when he was right for once, did he work so hard to put himself on the wrong side of the issue? The answer is that he himself did not believe a word he was saying. His anti-free trade rhetoric was for show only.

J. Duncan Edmonds, former chairman of the powerful lobbying group Public Affairs International, was a fervent free trader and believed that integration with the United States was inevitable. Beginning in 1978, Mr. Edmonds met regularly with Mr. Mulroney, and quickly came to the conclusion he had found a kindred spirit. When Mulroney then went on to denounce free trade in such inflamatory language, Mr. Edmonds was very surprised. **"It was a complete contradiction of what he said to me and what his view was, given his relationship with the Iron Ore Company".** (*Pledge of Allegiance*, Lawrence Martin, p. 45)

So when Brian Mulroney joined Ronald Reagan in a rendition of "When Irish Eyes are Smiling," and launched his free trade initiative, had he changed his mind? Or was he just revealing publically what his closest friends knew all along? Was he finally coming clean about where he really stood? With him and his colleagues one never knows.

At this time, we should remember not Prime Minister Mulroney, but candidate Mulroney, "québécois pure laine," because when he offered himself up as the saviour of the Progressive Conservative Party, he did so as the candidate who could break the Liberal Party's stranglehold on Quebec.

In the course of an interview given during dinner in his room at the Château Laurier Hotel in Ottawa, on May 23, 1983, Mr. Mulroney told a reporter from *La Presse:*

Vous parlez à un québécois pure laine, un québécois de Baie Comeau pure laine.

Though he described himself as "québécois pure laine" — a dyed-in-the-wool Quebecker — to a reporter in his hotel room, Mr. Mulroney went to great lengths to publicly disassociate himself from Quebec nationalists and even from Mr. Clark's constitutional position.

Thanks to Senator Murray, we know that Mr. Mulroney approved of Prime Minister Trudeau's earlier attempt to unilaterally patriate the Constitution, notwithstanding the vociferous objections of the Quebec government. In the book, *One Eyed Kings*, by Ron Graham, Senator Murray is quoted as having said:

> **Brian tends to be pretty simplistic when it comes to strategy, ...He goes for the big splash. He supported Trudeau's constitutional position not because he had thought about it for five minutes, but because he was so thrilled by the sheer bravado of it all. (p. 161)**

Not only did Mulroney support Mr. Trudeau's position in 1980, he actually praised him in 1983, endorsing his fight against Quebec separatism. Mr. Mulroney said: **"Pierre Trudeau is a Canadian who loves his country and he's a Quebecer trying to keep it (Canada) together."** (*Windsor Star*, June 4/83)

While agreeing with Prime Minister Trudeau's actions, Mulroney deliberately distanced himself from the approach taken by the leader of the Conservative Party, and former prime minister, Joe Clark. According to *Le Droit* of April 9/83, Mr. Mulroney

> *a refusé, vendredi, d'endosser la prise de position de son adversaire Joe Clark préconisant pour le Québec une compensation financière complète advenant que cette province se retire des amendements constitutionnels futurs.*

Later, according to *Le Devoir*,

> *M. Mulroney juge la position de son adversaire, M. Joe Clark «extrêmement dangeureuse» à ce sujet.* (April 26/83)

When not blasting away at his leading rival, Mr. Mulroney trained his sights on the separatists. **"I don't play footsy with the Parti Québécois,"** he said. (*Toronto Star*, April 24/83) He even attacked Joe Clark for allegedly accepting support from Québec separatists:

> **"That kind of situation is dangerous for the candidate, dangerous for the party he seeks to lead and dangerous for the country he seeks to unify. ...You don't get to be leader of this country by playing footsie with the Parti Québécois."** (*Calgary Herald*, Apr. 29/83)

THE CONSERVATIVE CANDIDATE WITH COMPASSION

When asked if any PQ members were working on his campaign, Mr. Mulroney's response, according to the same *Calgary Herald* article, was a flat out "**No.**"

If Mr. Mulroney was not prepared to practice the politics of appeasement when it came to separatists, what was he proposing for Québec? What were the specifics? The answer: there were no specifics.

> "**I want to know what's coming down the tube from the other side,**" **Mulroney said, refusing to say if he would even negotiate compensation.** (*Calgary Herald*, **April 29/83**)

There wasn't even any point in talking about these things while the separatist government of Premier René Lévesque remained in power in Québec.

> «*Il n'existe pas de formule qui puisse satisfaire un gouvernement séparatiste*», *a-t-il déclaré hier à la presse montréalaise.* (*Le Devoir*, May 2/83)

> "Get rid of the PQ," Mulroney said, "and as prime minister of Canada I'd negotiate constitutional peace with the people of Québec just like that....there's no way of ever pleasing the PQ because it's after one thing only: The dissolution of Canada." (*Montreal Gazette*, May 4/83)

He tried to assure sceptics by routinely claiming that as a labour lawyer, "**I've reaped peace - and that's exactly what you'll get from me in constitutional negotiations**" (*Gazette*, May 7/83). With some members of the media, this shallow response didn't strike a particularly responsive chord. But Mr. Mulroney refused to budge on the question of revealing a constitutional strategy:

> *Aux journalistes qui lui reprochaient de cacher sa véritable position constitutionnelle aux délégués conservateurs, M. Mulroney a répliqué qu'un bon stratège ne met jamais ses cartes sur table avant le début des négociations:* «*Ce sera la responsabilité du prochain chef; c'est complexe, il faut être prudent; ce n'est pas quelquechose que vous décidez un samedi soir sur la plate-forme arrière d'un camion*». (*Le Devoir*, May 2/83)

THE SHOW MUST NOT GO ON

However, one day after this statement of principle appeared in *Le Devoir*, Mr. Mulroney released a nine-point constitutional plan, which, he boasted to a Montreal reporter, he had drafted **"on the back of a Québecair barf bag on the flight from Quebec City to Mont Joli."** (*Montreal Gazette*, May 7/83)

More later on these themes of the deficit and constitutional reform. For the moment, on to another Mulroney theme, perhaps the one where he displayed his greatest eloquence, namely, patronage.

In addition to promising constitutional peace and a new prosperity, as well as integrity in government, Mr. Mulroney did not forget the need to stir the hearts of his Conservative workers.

> **Mr. Mulroney said the PCs will give the Liberals "their pink slip and their running shoes" in the next federal election.**
>
> **"We're going to put them back on the street," he continued, saying "We'll tell them to get a job like the rest of us."**
>
> **He said if he becomes prime minister he will call upon qualified Liberals and NDPers to fill government-appointed posts, but only after 15 years and "I can't find a breathing Conservative." (*Telegraph Journal*, May 9/83)**

That same message was delivered to the faithful in all parts of the country.

> **"I intend to appoint all sorts of Liberals and NDP to top, sensitive jobs...after I've been prime minister for 15 years and I can't find a living, breathing Conservative alive to do the job," Mulroney tells the Tory faithful. (*Toronto Star*, April 24/83)**

The *Montréal Gazette* of May 7/83 describes a scene where Mr. Mulroney is leaving a meeting at a hotel in Jonquière.

> **Mulroney ran smack into 30 Alcan workers on their way to a study session elsewhere in the hotel.**
>
> **Assessing the situation quickly, Mulroney threw his arm around the shoulders of the nearest man and announced cheerfully:**
>
> **"There, ladies and gentlemen, goes Canada's next Senate."**

THE CONSERVATIVE CANDIDATE WITH COMPASSION

Notwithstanding the bright prospects held before the eyes of potential delegates Mulroney's victory was not a certainty in late May of 1983. In a memo dated May 22, Mulroney's convention organizer, John Thompson, wrote his boss:

> "People are scared of your candidacy because a) they are scared off by your organization b) they don't trust you."

Explaining this lack of trust, Thompson pointed to certain defects:

> "1) image is fuzzy...not certain who you are and what you stand for...2) it is perceived that you are not your own man — that someone else is pulling the strings — Conrad Black or some big business organization — that someone who is always perfect (changing shirts, Christian Dior shirts, Ken Doll image) should be suspicious(sic); that you are opportunistic — here today gone tomorrow..." (*The Contenders*, Martin, Gregg and Perlin, p. 83)

Well, any lack of trust and the perception of Mulroney as a tool of big business were not then sufficiently developed to deny him the Tory leadership on June 12, 1983. That would come only with experience, and when it did, Thompson's description of Mulroney as an **"opportunist — here today gone tomorrow"** would echo when Canadians were deprived of the chance of passing direct judgment on Prime Minister Mulroney and his record in the 1993 election.

In the summer of 1983, however, that suspicion, that uneasiness and distrust of candidate Mulroney was submerged in a sea of hope by Canadians who wanted to believe what he said. In a leap of faith, delegates to the Progressive Party Leadership Convention in Ottawa elected the candidate of economic prosperity, integrity, constitutional peace, anti-free trade, and patronage par excellence. Little did they know that their faith was to be rewarded on only one of his promises. But in 1983, faith and hope were high.

3.

"JOBS, JOBS, JOBS" AND "SACRED TRUSTS" ON THE ROAD TO PARLIAMENT

MR. MULRONEY WAS CHOSEN LEADER of the Progressive Conservative Party, after promising constitutional peace, economic prosperity, no free trade, integrity in politics, patronage, pink slips and running shoes for "boggy brained civil servants," pink slips and running shoes for Liberals and pink slips and running shoes for any members of his own cabinet who failed on CFB Chatham. But all that would have to wait a bit. First he would have to win a seat in the House of Commons.

A vacant constituency was required. That was provided by Elmer Mackay of Central Nova, who obligingly resigned his seat. Mr. Mulroney declared himself a candidate, won the nomination, and off he went campaigning again, this time for the by-election on August 29, 1983.

His approach was similar to the one that had won him the leadership of the Conservative Party. He stressed Liberal values. He promised economic renewal. There was a major new campaign theme, as well as a number of new promises custom-made for the riding. It doesn't really matter as it turned out what promises he made; all were to be broken. But in 1983, the people of Central Nova and Atlantic Canada, like many other Canadians, took those promises seriously. For example, the *Chronicle-Herald* of July 13/83, dateline Trenton, ran a story that began:

> **The Progressive Conservative caucus will battle any move to reduce transportation subsidies on Atlantic Provinces manufactured goods, party leader Brian Mulroney pledged Tuesday. ...**

This was not simply something that was said to a reporter at the back of an airplane. It was said before more than 3,000 persons in the Trenton Community Rink. Mulroney said:

"JOBS, JOBS, JOBS" AND "SACRED TRUSTS"

> "If they do anything to the freight rates (subsidies), except to increase them, we will mount such an opposition ... that Gerry Regan will be forced to fly Air Canada economy class for the rest of his life."

A month later, same city, different rally, the *Chronicle-Herald* of August 17, 1983, reported:

> At a party rally here for the Aug. 29 by election, Mr. Mulroney offered a "guarantee" that a Conservative government under his leadership would not cut freight subsidies but would increase them instead.
>
> Atlantic Canada, under the terms of confederation is entitled to a "fair kick at the can" in terms of transportation costs, he told a questioner at the party rally.

Two weeks earlier, same city, same promise, as Mr. Mulroney toured the Hawker-Siddeley plant. He told Lonnie Reekie, a welder at the Trenton works:

> "...there have to be increased transportation subsidies so these plants can compete with those in central Canada. But the Liberals want to cut them.
>
> I tell you, there will be no cuts when the Conservatives get in...." (*Toronto Star*, Aug. 3/83)

He stood before this man, shook his hand, probably put his arm around his shoulder, looked him in the face and told him:

> "I tell you there will be no cuts when the Conservatives get in."

Mr. Reekie undoubtedly believed Mr. Mulroney. Likewise the 3,000 cheering supporters in the Trenton arena.

Atlantic Canadians know what Prime Minister Mulroney actually did to the *"At and East"* transportation subsidy program. They know how the Tory Caucus responded when ordered by the Prime Minister to vote it out of existence. They did what they were told! There is still the *Maritime Freight Rate Act* and the *Atlantic Region Freight Assistance Act*, but the subsidies under those programs have been cut. But that is for later — let's stay with our chronology.

-29-

While campaigning in Central Nova, Mr. Mulroney was careful to show that his interests were not limited to just one constituency.

> **"I would refer to DEVCO not so much as a business but a socio-economic instrument for Cape Breton,"** Mr. Mulroney said. **"Canada has an obligation to such instruments and I wouldn't cut back on DEVCO or Cape Breton's two heavy water plants until I could attract new industry into the region. High tech might be the answer."** (*Globe and Mail*, Aug. 17/83)

What happened to DEVCO and the two heavy water plants after Mr. Mulroney became Prime Minister? Let's wait until we reach the appropriate point in our chronology, but you can guess.

In addition to his specific pledge about freight subsidies, Mr. Mulroney unveiled in the Trenton Community Rink what was to become one of his major refrains, both in the 1983 by-election, and in the 1984 General Election:

> **"There are only three issues: jobs, jobs, jobs."** (*Chronicle-Herald*, July 13/83)

Yes, the famous **"jobs, jobs, jobs"** speech had its beginnings ten years ago in Trenton, Nova Scotia. The unemployed of that province and that community were among the first, if not the very first to hear this immortal Mulroneyism. They may have forgotten that honour, but probably not how Prime Minister Mulroney twice had his ministers introduce legislation to cut off their unemployment insurance benefits, and how Candidate Mulroney told the people of New Glasgow: **"To be content with an unemployment rate of 10 per cent is just short of criminal."** (*Chronicle-Herald*, Aug. 26/83)

The national unemployment rate now stands at over 11 per cent. In Central Nova, in 1983, **"jobs, jobs, jobs"** rolled off Mulroney's lips like a prayer, and the voters were believers. What did not roll off his lips quite so easily, however, were the words **"universal health care."**

1983 was the year that extra-billing by doctors became a major national issue and for Candidate Mulroney, it was an unwelcome intrusion in an otherwise uneventful campaign. When the Liberal Minister of Health and Welfare, Monique Begin, announced that

"JOBS, JOBS, JOBS" AND "SACRED TRUSTS"

she would be introducing measures to end the practice, Mr. Mulroney turned to slippery evasion tactics in order to avoid taking a position.

Let's begin with the *Toronto Star*, of July 28/83.

> A Conservative government would be "generous" to the provinces and doctors on the prickly issue of medicare, Tory leader Brian Mulroney says.
>
> But Mulroney refused yesterday to be more specific than that.
>
> "Generous means generous," he snapped when pressed by reporters to give details of the party's stance on medicare.
>
> Mulroney would not explain what the Tories would do about hospital user fees or extra billing by doctors, practices which Health Minister Monique Begin says are hurting universal medicare.
>
> "I've said what I have to say," Mulroney said.
>
> And he made clear that further attempts to pin him down on medicare will be useless....

Instead of disclosing his own plans, Mr. Mulroney attacked the Health Minister for her **"confrontational tactics with the provinces,"** which he said, were **"far from civilized."** He charged that the real problem was federal cutbacks on medicare, which **"have left the provinces holding the bag"** and **"scrounging"** for money.

Though this approach was not about to fly, he tried again the next day.

> "The root cause of the problem with medicare is that the Liberals have reneged on funding commitments to the provinces," Mulroney told reporters yesterday while campaigning for the Aug. 29 Central Nova by-election.
>
> The solution to medicare's problems would be to re-establish funding "in a positive and generous way," Mulroney said after a private luncheon with area doctors.

> But Mulroney would not say how much more money the provinces could expect from a Conservative government. Neither would he say what Conservatives would do about extra billing by doctors or hospital user fees.

Then, as usual, he attacked the Liberal government, charging: **"They want to fight an election on the backs of doctors and the poor."** (*Toronto Star*, July 29/83)

But no matter how often he repeated this message, it was met with scepticism. For Mulroney, the answer lay not in providing his own proposals, but in placing his hand over his heart and pledging allegiance to Canada's social programs.

> **"The Conservative party was for medicare, it is for medicare today and it will be for medicare tomorrow."** (*Toronto Star*, Aug. 4/83)

That same newspaper article also describes how Mr. Mulroney told a rally in New Glasgow **"that medicare is a 'sacred trust'."**

This is the first reference we have been able to find of Mr. Mulroney's use of these famous words, **"sacred trust"**, in reference to Canada's social programs — another distinction for the people of Nova Scotia. They were the first to hear those immortal words, **"jobs, jobs, jobs"**. They were the first to hear about the **"sacred trust."** But the voters of Central Nova were still short on faith, so Candidate Mulroney once again came out of his corner swinging. The following newspaper columns describe Mr. Mulroney's medicare offensive in the final weeks of the by-election campaign. Now was time for the big whopper.

> **Mulroney pledged a Tory government would provide sufficient funding for all existing health-care programs, including current dental care and prescription programs in Nova Scotia.**
>
> **"These programs are part and parcel of our citizenship,"** he said. (*Toronto Star*, Aug. 19/83)

> **While Ottawa had launched medicare on a 50/50 cost-sharing basis, Mr. Mulroney said the federal Liberals have drop-**

"JOBS, JOBS, JOBS" AND "SACRED TRUSTS"

ped their percentage, with the provinces "left holding the bag."

The Tory leader said he is prepared to pledge a federal government to "a fair share" of medicare costs, promising to restore cost-sharing to the "original plan." (*Chronicle-Herald*, Aug. 24/83)

A Conservative government would restore the original 50-50 split in medicare costs between the federal and provincial governments if elected to office, says Tory leader Brian Mulroney.

In some cases - such as in northern British Columbia, New Brunswick and Nova Scotia - the federal share would likely be even higher, said Mulroney. ...

"National health care is not a political issue," he said. "You're entitled to the same kind of quality services irrespective of place of residence.

"That may mean in certain cases a higher percentage than 50 per cent." (*Ottawa Citizen*, Aug. 24/83)

So there it was: bright promises for the people of Nova Scotia, indeed for all Canadians. If he became prime minister, Mr. Mulroney would fund medicare on a 50/50 cost-sharing basis with the provinces, and in some cases the federal government's share would be greater than 50%. These statements were made following a meeting with premiers John Buchanan, James Lee, and Richard Hatfield.

The press reported that the three premiers, all Conservatives, were pleased, though apparently they did not get any specific commitments.

"I don't think I needed any promises," Buchanan said. "I trust Mr. Mulroney. I know what his philosophy is. I know what his approach to government is. And I agree with it. His approach is what Nova Scotians say is 'on all fours' with mine." (*Ottawa Citizen*, Aug. 24/83)

THE SHOW MUST NOT GO ON

"**I trust Mr. Mulroney,**" Premier Buchanan said. Buchanan's trust in Mr. Mulroney may not have been misplaced, but the people of his province, unlike Senator Buchanan, were given very specific promises, and these promises dealt with increased federal health care funding. They were made by Mr. Mulroney in New Glasgow - in the Crocodile Room of the Peter Pan Motel.

And now an irresistible short fast-forward.

Conservative leadership candidate Kim Campbell says she is ready to preside over a new era in medicare, in which Canadians could be required to pay for medical services they use. (*Globe and Mail*, Apr. 30/93)

As a member of Mr. Mulroney's team, Ms. Campbell helped break the health care promises made by her team leader and her party. Now she says that far from strengthening the foundations of our health care system, she is prepared to begin dismantling them. The details of her proposals and of what Mulroney and his team actually did to medicare will have to wait until a later chapter.

There is almost enough material from every day of the Central Nova by-election campaign to warrant a separate chapter. Let's sum up with a few highlights.

When asked to comment on Premier Bill Bennett's deficit-cutting strategy in British Columbia, particularly as it applied to his treatment of the public service, Mr. Mulroney replied:

"...if you sign a collective agreement it must be presumed that you know what you're signing ... I've always contended that a document signed is a document to be honored."(*Vancouver Sun*, Aug. 10/83)

"I reject the approach that you can unilaterally change an agreement to the detriment of a co-signatory when you were under no obligation to sign it in the first place. ..." (*Globe and Mail*, Aug. 17/83)

What he rejected he did when it came time to deal with federal public servants.

"JOBS, JOBS, JOBS" AND "SACRED TRUSTS"

What were his views on the deficit?

"**You are not going to save this country from the financial and economic morass it is in simply by restraint. Restraint is fine, but you don't feed a family on six-and-five when you don't have a job. The most important question of priority is not restraint. It's unemployment.**" (*Vancouver Sun*, Aug. 10/83)

What about the principle of general elections every four years?

"**Prime Minister Trudeau is getting to the end of his four-year term, he is trying to establish a new constitutional principle, or custom, in Canada of a five-year term. This is another violation of British parliamentary traditions,...**" (*Vancouver Sun*, Aug. 10/83)

Mulroney, and his team and his successor have been in violation of Mulroney's own "principle" since November of 1992.

That the future Prime Minister of Canada would so mislead Canadians in 1983 no longer shocks. Over the years, we have become accustomed to distinguishing Mulroney fantasy from Mulroney reality. But what still shocks is the language the man who wanted to be Canada's Prime Minister used when attacking his political opponents.

A *Toronto Star* article, dated July 17, 1983, describes Mr. Mulroney's nomination meeting in Central Nova.

...Mulroney told the crowd of more than 3,500 that in any other "civilized country," MacEachen would by lynched for "ruining and devastating the country" when he was finance minister,...

The article goes on to say: "**...you could have heard a pin drop in the hockey rink. Mulroney, never one to miss a cue, quickly moved on to another topic.**"

Mr. Mulroney won the by-election on August 29/83. Now, 10 years later, after announcing his resignation, he will not venture back to Nova Scotia. Instead, he went abroad to those other "civilized countries", on a farewell tour, seeking respect and reassurance from foreign leaders.

4.

THE "HONORABLE" MEMBER FROM CENTRAL NOVA

ON ELECTION NIGHT, AT HIS ELECTION HEADQUARTERS in New Glasgow, Mr. Mulroney climbed onto the stage with his wife Mila, together with Elmer Mackay and Premier John Buchanan. They proceeded to entertain the crowd with a rendition of "When Irish Eyes are Smiling." When the singing was over, the newly-minted member for Central Nova proclaimed:

> "No party has done such damage to the soul of our nation as the Liberals. ...Tonight we begin the removal of a decaying, unprincipled group of people, replacing them with new people, new ideas and a majority government which will produce for you and for the benefit of your children a brand new Canada, ...Tonight we begin to make things better for all Canadians." (*Toronto Star/Toronto Sun*, Aug. 30/83)

It is a bit painful to read these words after all that has happened during the last ten years. These promises of **"new ideas"** and **"new people"**, and of a **"brand new"** and **"better"** Canada today are dead and buried in the bogs of fiscal incompetence, economic mismanagement and political corruption. That's what we see today in our rearview mirror. But in 1983, the view through the windshield of the road ahead was very different. It was a road that we wanted to believe would lead to prosperity. It was sold to us as a coast downhill.

In his first press interview following the by-election, Mr. Mulroney was asked by Richard Gwyn:

> "Everyone always says they will reduce the deficit by increasing economic growth. You are then deliberately making no commitment to reducing the budget deficit by spending restraint?" (*Toronto Star*, Aug. 31/83)

THE "HONORABLE" MEMBER FROM CENTRAL NOVA

What was Mr. Mulroney's response? Did he disagree with Mr. Gwyn? Did declare war on the deficit? No. He answered:

"Certainly there will be restraint. But spending cuts will be fairly modest, a reduction in the rate of increase of spending."

These words disclose no preoccupation, not even serious concern with the deficit. There would be some "modest" spending cuts, but government spending would continue to increase. Rather than talk about the deficit, there was more interest in conveying to voters the image of a Conservative government imbued with compassion and understanding. Mulroney continued:

"The fact is, we've devised in Canada a structure of social programs that in many ways serves us very well."

"We've devised..." said the new leader of the Conservative Party. It was not Mr. Mulroney, working for the Iron Ore Company of Cleveland, Ohio, nor his Conservative friends who devised these programs; rather it was successive Liberal governments. Liberal governments devised these programs, and Liberal governments implemented them, so as governments, it was they who had served Canadians very well.

"Some people might like to chop at it. But this isn't going to happen. We are not Britain. We are not the United States. Those social programs do honor to the character of the country."

There would be no chopping. **"... this isn't going to happen"**, Mulroney promised. Well, it did happen. The family allowance program was chopped. It's gone, as is the Child Tax Credit and the Income Tax deduction for the cost of raising children. When income tax forms are filled out next year, there will be a place to deduct the cost of private boxes at Sky Dome, but no place to deduct the cost of raising children.

Old age pensioners almost got the chop. Instead, when scared off by the people, Mr. Mulroney and friends invented the "claw back."

What about the Unemployment Insurance Program? No mercy there either. It has certainly received more than its fair share of whacks from this Lizzie Borden government.

Now, Tory Leader Kim Campbell, looking for new victims, scrambles to cut and bleed our health care system. During the 1993 Tory leadership race, it was a contest to see which Tory candidate could promise to do the most chopping on what's left of our social programs, the remains of the very same programs that Mr. Mulroney described in 1983 as doing **"honor to the character of the country."** But that is today. In 1983, Canadians knew only the promises and assurances of a Conservative leader decked out in Liberal clothing. They only knew the leader who had solemnly pledged that the universality of social programs was **"a cornerstone of our party's philosophy."** (*Globe and Mail,* March 24/84) They could not see the axe which was being secretly sharpened for use after the general election.

Even when he was asked directly, face to face, on a television interview: **"What about the safety nets - the social services?"**, Mulroney didn't flinch. Like a good gambler, he looked pokerfaced into the camera and said:

> **"That is a moral obligation that we have as a country but we can maintain that moral fabric of the country with no problem - none whatsoever to the elderly, to the dispossessed, the disadvantaged, to the unemployed. This is a moral capacity of Canada that we must honour at all times..."**
> (*CHCH-TV, Hamilton, The Cherington Show,* Apr. 30/84)

Experience has taught the unemployed, the elderly, the dispossessed and the disadvantaged, many of whom saw that interview, to check their wallets when any member of the Mulroney team talks about "moral" obligations. For them, it has been a painful experience.

On March 22, 1984, Mr. Mulroney told the Montreal Chamber of Commerce:

> **"I want to be able to say that I live in a society where poverty has been eliminated; where the basic needs of all citizens**

are provided for; where one can grow old without growing poor." (*Montreal Gazette*, March 23, 1984)

Mr. Mulroney can hardly say that nine years later. Recently, a band of his supporters in the House of Commons got together to examine poverty income levels. They concluded that the income levels Statistics Canada uses to define poverty are too high. If those income levels were reduced, presto, government statistics would show fewer people living in poverty. I suppose that if they were reduced enough, poverty could be "officially" eliminated. A neat solution for everyone except the poor.

But what about the deficit? How would the new member from Central Nova Mr. Mulroney deal with it? When the head of the M-team was questioned about the deficit, he replied:

"The answer to reducing the deficit will not come from cosmetic cuts or changes. It has to be a totally re-energized economy based principally on new trust and new confidence, by new strength in the private sector and enhanced productivity, doubling of our commitment to research and development...." (*CTV Question Period*, Dec. 18/83)

Once again, a revitalized economy would take care of the deficit. In his answer, there was no mention whatsoever of any spending cuts. In fact, there would be even less government revenues to deal with the deficit because there would be new tax breaks for research and development. There would also be new expenditures.

In the House of Commons, the new member called for **"a massive manpower retraining program.... There must be a massive commitment, in co-operation with labour, management and government, to the development of the most thoughtful and generous manpower retraining program a civilized society has ever put together."** (*Hansard*, Dec. 9/83, p. 43)

A massive training program — so massive, that it would be the most generous in the civilized world is what Mr. Mulroney promised. There was, of course, no massive retraining program.

In fact, when we come to examine Mr. Wilson's budgets, we will find cuts to existing training programs. In 1983 and 1984, what

Mulroney was building for Canadians was a facade, not a building. The facade included increased expenditures for defence:

> "**This is a first class country and we're going to go first class in the area of conventional defence - under a new Progressive Conservative government....**
>
> **We are going to do it first class — first class equipment, deployment capacity, and first class wages....** "(*CHCH TV Hamilton, the Cherington Show* - April 30/84)

That has not happened. In fact, increases in defence expenditures actually slowed with the election of a Conservative government. More recently, there have been reports that our troops in Bosnia are at risk because of second-rate equipment. But that is today — in 1984, there was a facade to be built.

Back to the deficit. Under Mulroneyomics, our version of Reaganomics, we were going to have increased spending for R&D, increased spending for defence, as well as a massive retraining program. Program spending would not be slashed because social programs were a "sacred trust". Would a Conservative government increase taxes to make up the difference? For the answer, let's turn to the words of the man to whom Mr. Mulroney would entrust the economy, Mr. Michael Wilson. He said:

> "**We would not raise taxes. Tax levels in Canada are already too high.**" (*Hansard,* March 6/84, p. 1827)

Those words were spoken 39 or 40 tax increases ago. In 1984, tax levels, according to Mr. Wilson — the same Mr. Wilson who now supports Ms. Campbell because he is satisfied she will carry on his works — were "already too high." Nine years and forty tax increases later, what about the deficit? In Michael Wilson's first budget in 1985, it was $34.5 billion. In Mr. Mazankowski's most recent budget, it was $35.5 billion. An increase of $1 billion!

What about the economy — what miracles would the Mulroney-Wilson team work there? Unfortunately, they would be very similar to the kind of magic they worked on the government's finances.

THE "HONORABLE" MEMBER FROM CENTRAL NOVA

Let's start with this article from the *St. John's Evening Telegram*, of June 15, 1984 - dateline, Corner Brook:

> **Mulroney said his party can do great things for Newfoundland and Labrador.**
>
> **"I'm going to burden Newfoundlanders with prosperity and I think they are going to wear prosperity well," he said.**

He got the verb right. He certainly did "burden" Newfoundlanders, but was it with prosperity? Who in Newfoundland now staggers under the burden of prosperity? In 1983, and 1984, however, no statement was too outrageous for Mr. Mulroney where the economy or his own abilities were concerned. In a March 24, 1984, interview with the *Financial Post*, he said: **"look at this country. It's belly-up"**. That same month, his future Minister of Finance, Michael Wilson, complained:

> **"The growth of our national economy in the fourth quarter of 1983 was only .9 per cent, after being adjusted for inflation. That expressed on an annual basis is 3.6 per cent..."** (*Hansard*, March 6/84, p. 1827)

"Only" .9 per cent in the fourth quarter, Wilson moaned. What have been the increases in the last 12 quarters, after being adjusted for inflation? The answer, starting with the 1st quarter of 1990, is 0.7; 0.1; minus 0.7; minus 2.0; minus 3.6; minus 1.9; minus 1.2; 0.0; 1.5; 0.3; 0.4; and 1.3. In only two of the last 12 quarters was .9% GDP growth exceeded by the Mulroneyites.

In 1983, GDP increased 3.2 per cent. In 1984, GDP increased 6.3%. Those were the terrible Liberal years Mulroney and Wilson were complaining they were stuck with. In 1990, GDP <u>decreased</u> 0.5 per cent. In 1991, it <u>decreased</u> 1.7 per cent. In 1992, it skyrocketed by 0.9% — that is <u>0.9</u> per cent for the entire year! These are the fruits of nine Conservative years, years for which Mulroney, and Wilson, and Mazankowski, and Campbell want Canadians to thank them and ask for more.

So much for the deficit and the economy. What about the Constitution? We have already seen how candidate Mulroney had studiously crafted his constitutional program on a Québecair barf-bag, as he called it. Was Mr. Mulroney, the member from Central Nova, preoccupied by the separatist threat in Quebec? In late 1983, was he lamenting how Quebec had been humiliated and left sitting on the snowbank when the Constitution had been patriated over the objections of its separatist government, led by Premier René Lévesque? Was he warning that separatist sentiment was running wild through the streets of Quebec, threatening to destroy the country unless immediate steps were taken to heal the grievous wounds inflicted by Prime Minister Trudeau? Was the separation of Quebec even a concern of his? According to his own words, the answer is "No."

While in Epiphanie, Quebec, to honour M.P. Roch LaSalle, Mr. Mulroney claimed that the possible separation of Quebec was not an issue:

"By their referendum response (60 per cent of voters turned down the Parti Quebecois' proposal to negotiate sovereignty association) Quebecers have put an end to the question of separation", Mulroney said. "As far as I'm concerned, the debate is closed." (*Chronicle-Herald*, Sept. 6/83)

These words of the future Prime Minister were not helpful to ministers who later were placed in charge of federal-provincial relations, in particular, Senator Lowell Murray and the Right Honourable Joe Clark. To transform what Mr. Mulroney called a closed debate into a national crisis paralyzing the country required real talent. Unfortunately for Canadians, the Mulroney government had plenty of demagogic talent. And whenever there was a shortage, more talented individuals were found, even if it meant scouring our embassies overseas to find separatist alarmists.

No matter how much Senator Murray and Mr. Clark may now deny it, Mr. Mulroney had it right in 1983. The constitutional trauma which followed was the direct result of pursuing partisan political objectives at all costs, even at the cost of national unity. But that is an episode which will have to wait until we are well into the record of the Mulroney team's administration. For now, we are

THE "HONORABLE" MEMBER FROM CENTRAL NOVA

still dealing with Mr. Mulroney, the new member from Central Nova, prime minister in waiting.

Canadians, of course, wondered, how this businessman, for whom politics was but a recreation, would perform when thrown to the lions in the House of Commons. Mr. Mulroney took his seat on September 12, 1983. The following day, during question period, he took a shot at the Minister of Health, asking her when she was expecting to give birth, knowing she was not pregnant and not married. Less than two weeks later, he was in Pictou County, telling his constituents that his biggest surprise in the Commons was the **"total lack of civility"** of the Liberals. (*Chronicle-Herald*, Sept. 26/83) Back in the House of Commons, when a Parliamentary Secretary rose in the absence of the Minister to respond to his question, Mr. Mulroney said: **"I want to hear it from the organ grinder and not the monkey."** (*Hansard*, Nov. 21/83, p. 29022) The new boy with a new, higher standard of civility!

These incidents are minor, but they are instructive; they provide an early indication of something that turned out to be far more important, namely, what Mr. Mulroney really thought of Parliament. They also provide the beginnings of an explanation for the poisonous atmosphere which existed in the House of Commons throughout his administration.

Though Mr. Mulroney was more than willing to smear Liberals at every available opportunity, he himself was very sensitive to any criticism or scrutiny. In fact, his thin skin led directly to one of the more bizarre episodes in Canadian politics.

On February 15, 1984, the *Globe and Mail* ran a story alleging that staff in the Office of the Prime Minister was engaged in a secret intelligence gathering mission, to uncover incriminating material on Mr. Mulroney while he was President of the Iron Ore Company of Canada. Question period that day was dominated by the story. There were charges of law-breaking, improper use of public funds, Watergate-type spying and requests for an independent inquiry. But when all was said and done, what emerged was the story of a summer student working away at the University of Ottawa Library researching the layoffs in Schefferville. There was also a staff member in the PMO who, while in Washington,

THE SHOW MUST NOT GO ON

dropped into the offices of the Securities and Exchange Commission to get a copy of Iron Ore Company's annual report, a public document.

Media representatives were invited into the Prime Minister Trudeau's office to look at the dossier compiled on Mulroney. It consisted of 10 file folders of newspaper clippings and one binder of public documents on the Iron Ore Company. (*Toronto Star*, Feb. 16/84)

When reporters asked to see the files Mulroney's office kept on Trudeau, they were first refused, and then only reluctantly shown not ten file folders of clippings, but 10 filing drawers of material, which included, according to the *Toronto Star* of February 17, 1984, **"claims that Trudeau is everything from a Communist to a capitalist lackey."** There were also files on John Turner, who was not even a Member of Parliament at that time, but **"Fred Doucet, Mulroney's Chief of Staff, refused to allow reporters to view the Turner material, saying the media had been allowed into Tory research offices only to see the Trudeau files."** (*Toronto Star*, Feb. 17/84)

When this issue was before the House of Commons, not only did it dominate Question Period, but it was the subject of a Question of a Privilege raised by Mr. Mulroney's House Leader, Erik Neilsen. On February 15, 1984, Mr. Neilsen alleged that the incident **"is a very grave and probably the most serious matter to have come before the House, certainly in my experience ...Surely this is one of the most serious revelations ever to come before a House of Commons in any parliamentary democracy."** (*Hansard*, pages 1415-6). He went on to say: **"Individual members of the House should not be subject to... invasion of privacy simply because the Government finds it expedient to engage in such practices."** (p. 1419)

Yes, that's the same Mr. Neilsen, delivering an indictment which had no basis in fact, who previously had spent countless hours eavesdropping on the private deliberations of National Liberal Caucus. This, however, was not known to Canadians at the time. It would not be revealed until some time after the election. In early 1984, Canadians could only see the righteous Mr. Neilsen, the right-hand man of Mr. Mulroney, condemning the Liberal government for collecting newspaper clippings on his boss. Not revealed was Neilsen hunched over, in some darkened room, electronically eavesdropping on the private meetings of Liberal Caucus, eavesdropping on the private meetings of Members of Parliament.

How is that for hypocrisy? What did Mr. Mulroney do and say when his deputy's activities finally were revealed? The answer will be provided in due course.

We have already seen how Mr. Mulroney donned the cloak of liberalism when campaigning for office. That cloak remained wrapped around his shoulders as the new member from Central Nova. In the House of Commons, Mr. Mulroney again spoke of "tenderness":

> "There is ... the obligation to show tenderness towards underprivileged Canadians. It is an altogether sacrosanct obligation towards the poor, the underprivileged and the elderly. It is also an absolutely essential aspect of our national character." (*Hansard*, Dec. 9/83, p. 45)

Nor had he not forgotten the sanctity of medicare:

> "As far as the Conservative Party is concerned, medicare is a sacred trust which we will always preserve. ... There must be certain things that are above politics - there are certain things in Canada which must be safeguarded against any partisan attack - Medicare has to be one of them at all times." (*Hansard*, Dec. 9/83, p. 44)

Were these words read back in 1993 to the contenders for his job? In 1984, Mr. Mulroney had advice for Mr. Trudeau about contenders:

> "We want to know how much disintegration can Trudeau tolerate before he has to respond by dismissing ministers who repudiate government policy. ...They (the Liberal leadership contenders) are desperately trying to repudiate the government they served so loyally... Basic honor calls for resignations." (*Gazette*, April 9/84)

In 1984, the policy issue which incensed Mr. Mulroney was the future of Petro Canada gas stations. In early 1993, the policy issue was the future of medicare.

No one has ever described gas stations as **"a sacred trust which we will always preserve"**. But Mr. Mulroney used those very words to describe medicare. Prime Minister Mulroney's would-be successors, including his cabinet ministers Campbell and Charest, were all saying they would end universality for medicare. If that was not government policy, were not Mr. Mulroney's words of 1984 appropriate: **"Basic honor calls for resignations."**

Speaking of gas stations, this is a good time to recall what Mr. Mulroney had in mind for Petro-Canada. Would a Conservative government dismantle or sell the Crown Corporation? Looking at the situation today, is Petro-Canada for sale? The answer is yes. Legislation to privatize Petro-Canada has been passed and the government is now waiting for an opportunity to enter the stock market with Petro-Canada shares. This might be a good time to test a hypothesis for which we already have seen much evidence, namely "the contrary-performance" rule. If that rule was followed by Mr. Mulroney we can be sure that Mr. Mulroney promised not to sell Petro-Canada. That would be a reasonable inference from everything we have seen. If Petro Canada is now for sale, at some time Mulroney must have said that it would not be for sale. Well, what are the facts?

Let's start with *La Presse* of April 9, 1984:

Le chef conservateur, Brian Mulroney, croit à l'utilité de Pétro-Canada comme institution nationale et il n'a pas l'intention de démanteler cette société de la Couronne si son parti forme le prochain gouvernement. ... «Pétro-Canada est une institution nationale que je garderai intacte», a-t-il dit en réponse à plusieurs questions des journalistes sur ce sujet.

The *Toronto Star* of that same date reported:

... Mulroney angrily dodged reporters' questions yesterday about what a Tory government would do with the crown-owned oil company.

...The Tory leader reacted testily to persistent questioning about what his party's policy is on Petro-Canada, a major issue in the 1980 election when the Conservatives vowed to privatize the company.

THE "HONORABLE" MEMBER FROM CENTRAL NOVA

"We don't propose to dismantle it," Mulroney said, adding: "I don't propose to comment on silly and self-serving comments, which change every day, by Liberal leadership candidates."

A few days later, on the CBC Radio program *"The House"*, the following exchange took place.

CBC: "Would you sell part of Petro-Canada?"

Mulroney: "Look, I, you know, that's the silliest thing that has come up." (April 14, 1984)

So our hypothesis is correct. We have found several statements by Mr. Mulroney, all promising not to sell Petro-Canada. In retrospect, one might have thought that the oil company was safe, for not once did Mr. Mulroney call it a "sacred trust". Well, one would have been wrong. What Mr. Mulroney characterized as "silly" became government policy. Petro-Canada is on the block for privatization.

Will our hypothesis prove true in other cases? Will it work for Air Canada? We know that the Mulroney government sold-off Air Canada. It is now a private company. Our hypothesis, therefore, predicts that Mr. Mulroney must have promised not to sell Air Canada. Once again, research confirms the validity of the hypothesis. In an interview given to *The Financial Post*, Mr. Mulroney made it clear that the company would not be sold:

"Air Canada is being well run now, it's being run according to private-sector economics and criteria to the extent humanly possible. It pays down its debt, it has productivity enhancement programs, it shows from time to time a small profit, it has management that seems to be concerned about the bottom line, so I'm reasonably impressed." (March 24, 1984)

This hypothesis' merit is its unerring accuracy. Look at government policy today, and you can be sure that Mr. Mulroney promised the exact opposite. If only Canadians had known about "contrary performance" in 1984! We have already seen many examples apart from Petro-Canada and Air Canada. Today, we have a free trade deal with the United States. The hypothesis predicts that Mr. Mulroney promised no free trade. As we saw earlier, that is exactly what he promised.

Today we have soaring unemployment. That must mean he must have promised jobs. Sure enough, he promised "jobs, jobs, jobs."

Today we have a soaring deficit. That must mean a balanced budget was promised. We have already seen that it was.

Today we have an economy on the ropes. That must mean a dynamic and surging economy was promised. Sure enough, it was.

Today we have wholly inadequate expenditures on Research and Development. That must mean there was a promise from Mr. Mulroney to increase, and even to double R&D expenditures. That is exactly what was promised.

Our social programs have either been eliminated or eroded. That must mean there was a commitment from Mr. Mulroney to treat them as a sacred trust. Was there? Yes, yes. Every Canadian knows there was.

Over the years, Mr. Mulroney has, in an orgy of patronage, appointed favoured *friends* to virtually every government body in the country. That must mean that he promised appointments to total *strangers* on the street. We have seen that is exactly what he did on the streets of Jonquière.

This is uncanny. We have an hypothesis that, so far, is 100% verified. The man and his party have established a record of complete reliability: they will do the opposite of what they say they'll do. That's something to remember in Campaign '93.

But let's continue with our examination of Mr. Mulroney and see if he managed to maintain his unblemished record of "contrary performance."

While Leader of the Opposition, Mr. Mulroney promised that a Conservative Government would usher in a new era for the women of Canada:

"A Progressive Conservative Government will ensure that all companies seeking to provide services to the Government of Canada hire increasing numbers of women to per-

form those services as a condition of getting the job," Mr. Mulroney said. "We will ask those firms to show us, as part of their tendering responsibilities, how many women will be hired to fulfil those contracts." (*Globe and Mail,* March 5/84)

This statement was made to the Progressive Conservative Women's National Caucus. According to the *Ottawa Citizen* of March 5/84, **"Mulroney also promised the women's caucus pensions for homemakers."**

Ms. Janis Johnson — now Senator Johnson — then the Director of the Conservative Party, declared that Mulroney had delivered **"a profound speech"** and that the party was **"moving forward in a tremendous direction"** (*Toronto Star,* March 5/84). We know that these promises were not kept. Senator Janis Johnson knows there is no homemakers pension. Senator Johnson now knows there is no requirement in the tendering process for any indication of how many women would be hired to fulfil a contract. As usual with Mr. Mulroney the "profound" turned out to be shallow.

Mr. Mulroney also promised housing assistance for those in need.

Nous devons veiller à ce que notre régime fiscal soit juste et équitable et à ce que nos dépenses fiscales et nos programmes dans des domaines comme l'aide à l'habitation soient soigneusement ajustés pour profiter à ceux qui en ont vraiment besoin. (Le Devoir, **Mar. 23/84)**

There must no longer be any Canadians in need of housing assistance or any homeless people, for on April 26, 1993, Finance Minister Mazankowski announced: **"CMHC will no longer fund housing through 35-year subsidy commitments."**

That announcement, on page 10 of his budget, was the culmination of five years of slashing federal spending on social housing. The hypothesis scores again!

Mr. Mulroney promised a new role for parliamentarians. He spoke approvingly about the

"...creation of a joint Senate and House of Commons standing committee on crown corporations, with the mandate

and resources to undertake effective cyclical reviews of individual corporations." (*Toronto Star,* Feb. 24/84)

Parliamentarians are still waiting.

A week after promising this new responsibility for the Senate, he was unveiling a somewhat different notion in Nova Scotia.

A Conservative government might abolish the Upper Chamber of Parliament, Tory leader Brian Mulroney told an audience of high school students here Friday. "We're going to change it (the Senate) dramatically or we're going to get rid of it," Mr. Mulroney said... "As things stand now, the Upper Chamber is little more than a 'retirement home' for a bunch of Grits." (*Chronicle-Herald,* Mar. 31/84)

Did Mr. Mulroney get rid of the Senate? No. In fact, since 1984, he has had more than 50 new senators marched down the aisle. Did he change the Senate dramatically? Perhaps we here have a promise that was kept, but in an unanticipated way.

First, in 1990, he sent an urgent message to Her Majesty, Queen Elizabeth II, asking for Tory reinforcements to secure passage of his beloved GST in the Senate. He told her that the Liberals were engaged in systemic obstruction. As a result eight new Tory senators were added.

When that failed to get the GST passed, a new strategy was devised. Conservative senators signed a letter, addressed to Mulroney's old friend and fund raiser, Speaker Guy Charbonneau, asking for an immediate vote on the GST. Never mind that this would mean breaking the rules and traditions of the Senate. Charbonneau agreed. The vote was held. And Canadians got the GST for Christmas.

And then finally to put the Senate's neck totally under the government's boot, the Tory senators used their majority unilaterally to rewrite the Senate Rule book, eliminating any possibility of effective opposition to Mulroney's program.

The Mulroney team <u>did</u> change the Senate. It changed it dramatically. In a manner of speaking, here is one Mulroney promise that was kept, but kept in a way that infuriated most

Canadians. His treatment of the Senate raised the ire of even some of the leading members of his team, including one of his former ministers, the Hon. Pat Carney.

> **Carney said Mulroney entreated her to take the Senate appointment because he needed her B.C. expertise, then turned around and publicly talked about abolishing it. "He trashed the Senate even as he was appointing people to it. I think that's hypocritical."** (*Vancouver Sun*, June 30/93)

These are harsh words from a former member of Mulroney's inner circle - harsh but accurate.

We will close this chapter with a short word about a favorite Mulroney topic, patronage.

We already have seen how Mr. Mulroney promised pink slips for Liberals and bonbons for Conservatives while campaigning for the leadership of the Conservative Party and for election in Central Nova. But once he had become a Parliamentarian, a more dignified approach was called for. No more Senate seats for strangers on the street. From now on, patronage would only be mentioned in the most dignified, lofty tones.

On CTV's *Question Period*, June 24, 1984, Mr. Mulroney said:

> **"I will acknowledge that the vulgarity of the Liberal patronage machine is such that we're all going to have to take a second look at our partisanship. I think there is going to have to be coming from us, from a new government, an effort - not only an effort, a determination - to get away from it once and for all, and that is going to require some dramatic moves by me to cut down on that."**

He certainly did make some dramatic moves that gave patronage a whole new meaning, but that is for later. On July 9, 1984, Parliament was dissolved and an election was called for September 4. Mr. Mulroney was off and running and promising. He intended to talk Canadians into making him Prime Minister of Canada.

5.

"YOU HAD AN OPTION" — ELECTION 84

TO BEGIN OUR EXAMINATION of Mr. Mulroney's performance during the 1984 general election campaign, we'll start where we left off in Part 4 and wrap up, for now, the subject of patronage.

The first scene is the CTV Studio in Ottawa, on July 25, 1984.

Mulroney: You had an option, sir. You could have said,"I am not going to do it. This is wrong for Canada, and I'm not going to ask Canadians to pay the price." You had an option, sir, to say, no, and you chose to say yes to the old attitudes and the old stories of the Liberal Party. That, sir, if I may say respectfully, that is not good enough for Canadians.

Turner: I had no option. I was...

Mulroney: That is an avowal of failure. That is a confession of non-leadership and this country needs leadership. You had an option, sir. You could have done better.

That exchange on patronage between Turner and Mulroney was a crucial point in the election campaign. It was the culmination of a series of attacks that Mr. Mulroney launched against Mr. Turner on the very day the election campaign began. When the general election was called on Monday, July 9, 1984, Mr. Mulroney immediately called a press conference. After characterizing prior Liberal appointments as **"shameful"**, **"vulgar"**, and **"a scandal"**, he solemnly declared:

"I commit myself as a new Prime Minister to make a historical gesture — to clean up once and for all the similar appointment of people to high positions. Never will you see the application of this shameful and scandalous gesture.«

If nominations are to be made for the new government..., you will be impressed by the quality and the impartiality with which we will appoint people to those positions. ...I

undertake today that all political appointments will be of the highest unimpeachable quality. I'm going to send out a dramatic signal of renewal in this area of Canadian life."

Then one of the reporters asked: "Are you prepared to make these appointments by going through an office other than the Prime Minister's Office or some other quarter?"

He replied:

"Yes, that would be possible. I make this commitment before you and before the Canadian people. I commit myself to set up criteria for quality which will impress the Canadian people."

These quotations are from a transcript of the press conference.

Today, nine years later, Canadians know from experience what Mr. Mulroney meant when he said **"I make this commitment before you and before the Canadian people"**. They now know Mr. Mulroney's real agenda was not the one he tried to put past them while giving solemn undertakings and commitments. The real Mulroney was the one who chatted with reporters on the campaign plane en route to Montreal from Baie Comeau on Saturday, July 14, 1984. Just five days after making solemn declarations on national television to all Canadians, he told the gang in the back of the plane:

"Let's face it: there's no whore like an old whore. If I'd been in Bryce's position, I'd have been right in there with my nose in the public trough like the rest of them". (*Ottawa Citizen*, July 16/84)

His reference was to Bryce Mackasey's appointment as ambassador to Portugal.

Reporters were, of course, surprised by this unexpected burst of candour. They asked Mr. Mulroney how he could reconcile his various statements on patronage, including those made during the Conservative leadership campaign, when he said he would give a job to a Liberal only **"when there isn't a living breathing Tory left without a golden retirement."** His response was enlightening:

THE SHOW MUST NOT GO ON

"I was talking to Tories then, and that's what they want to hear. Talking to the Canadian public during an election campaign is something else."

As this chat in the back of the plane was winding down, Mr. Mulroney said:

"I hope this is all off the record. I'm taking the high road now."

Sure enough, less than two weeks later, Mulroney lambasted Turner over the patronage issue in the televised Leaders' Debate. He strode up his phony high road to victory. Soon thereafter he began welcoming his friends, who, came scurrying down the low road to patronage heaven.

Who were his friends? Perhaps we will never know who they all were. When it comes to patronage, or even appearances of patronage, friendship is not something that Conservatives find easy to talk about. Jean Charest, now Deputy Prime Minister, was no different during the PC leadership campaign.

In May of this year, it was revealed that Mr. Charest's campaign manager, Mr. David Small, had received $200,000 in untendered government contracts from Mr. Charest's own department. According to the *Ottawa Citizen* of May 20, 1993, the contracts came from **"the federal Environment Department and were for the polishing and promotion of Charest's image and that of his department"**. According to the same report, **"Charest later refused to say whether he and David Small are friends."**

Whether he refused three times to say that Mr. Small was his friend is not recorded. If they are friends, why this reluctance to admit it from the member of the Mulroney team who prides himself on candour? But back to Charest's mentor and leader, Brian Mulroney.

Mr. Mulroney, of course, apologized for his injudicious remarks on the campaign plane. He said that the Liberal appointments were so "vulgar" that it was time for everyone to reassess their positions.

"...a new government will never resort to this kind of attitude ... our proposals and our nominations will hopefully be

subject to vetting in advance". (*Ottawa Citizen*, July 19, 1984)

Well his hopes weren't met, unless what he meant by **"vetting in advance"** was that he himself would do the vetting. Nine years later, the Mulroney team repeats the same promise. This time its Kim Campbell who says that a conservative government will vet patronage appointments. New leader, same party, same promise, same story. At a rally, Mulroney said:

...I pledge to you here today that our appointments shall be of the highest quality. They ...shall bring honor to all of you and shall bring honor to this country. (*Globe and Mail*, July 23, 1984)

Enough for now about patronage. Later while examining the actual record of the Mulroney government, we may highlight some of the more interesting patronage appointments, and measure them against the standard Mr. Mulroney promised: appointments **"of the highest unimpeachable quality"** which would **"impress the Canadian people"** and **"bring honor to this country."**

Although we may remember best the patronage issue, the 1984 campaign, also featured substantive promises by the Tory leader. These promises, however, do not as readily spring to mind partly because they fall into the category of promises made to be broken. They were made, they were broken, they vanished. Let's revive them briefly.

In July 1984, the Conservative Party released a document entitled *"On the Issues - Brian Mulroney and the Progressive Conservative Agenda - Statements of Policy and Principle."* We've learned that when we see the name "Brian Mulroney" linked to the words "statements of policy and principle", that we are in for some bizarre reading. We are not disappointed.

At page 17 of the document, under the heading "Retraining Canada's Workforce", Mr. Mulroney says:

"We shall create a registered training account, — an R.T.A. — which would allow individuals to accumulate savings which could be invested in their own development."

Turning to pages 36 and 37 of the *PC Campaign Handbook*, which was carried like a Bible by Tory candidates during the summer of 1984, we read:

> **"We will set up a tax-sheltered savings plan (similar to a registered retirement plan) that will allow individuals to invest in their own education and training. Money invested in this personal Registered Training Plan (RTP) would be tax-exempt if used for educational purposes."**

Let us move ahead to *The Financial Post* of May 27, 1993.

> **The environment minister again promised strong emphasis on education and training. Up to $1,000 of annual savings for education would be exempt from federal taxes under a Charest-led government, he said.**

Should anyone be surprised that Mr. Charest in 1993 made the same promise which Mr. Mulroney made in 1984? Of course not. Charest is a leading member of the Conservative party as reconstituted by Mulroney. As a member of cabinet, he helped Mr. Mulroney break that promise, so why shouldn't he have the right to make it again?

As mentioned, this promise was contained in the *PC Campaign Handbook*, the handbook Charest undoubtedly used when selling Conservative Party policy to the people of Sherbrooke during the 1984 general election. The introduction to the *Handbook* states:

> **This Campaign Handbook has been prepared to assist you in taking the issues of this election campaign to the people in your constituency.**

Mr. Charest took the policies contained in the *Handbook* to his constituency. He was elected, became a member of Cabinet, and then helped Mr. Mulroney repudiate those policies. Then, with a straight face, he resurrects, temporarily, the very same policies he helped bury. This is easier than explaining why he helped kill them in the first place.

Let's continue with Mr. Mulroney's 1984 flood of promises. As we do, it is tempting to do nothing but rely on the *1984 PC Campaign Handbook*. That, however, would be much too easy. You simply open up the *Handbook*, read a sentence, and *voilà*, you have a broken promise. For instance, if you turn to page 72, you find the words **"We will increase the use of the work done by the Economic Council of Canada...."** That was what the Mulroney team promised. It was the death sentence for the Council! On page 130 of Mr. Mazankowski's first budget, we read: **"...legislation will be introduced to wind up the Economic Council."** Legislation was introduced, it was pushed through, and the Council was abolished. That is how the Mulroney Team kept that particular promise. If only we had known about "contrary performance"!

On page 60 of the *Handbook*, we read: **"A P.C. Government would once more index the Old Age Pension to the actual cost of living on a quarterly basis."**

How was that promise kept? For the answer, turn to page 17 of Michael Wilson's first budget:

"I propose to modify indexation for old age security payments..., beginning January 1, 1986, these payments will be indexed only for the annual increase in the consumer price index greater than 3 per cent."

Later Mr. Mulroney backed down after an irate pensioner told him **"Good-bye Charlie Brown"**, but Wilson revealed how Mulroney and the reconstituted Tory party intended to keep that particular promise.

Let's turn to page 62 of the *PC Campaign Handbook*. There we read:

"We will strengthen and expand co-operative housing programs."

How did the Mulroney team strengthen and expand co-operative housing? For the answer, turn to page 83 of Mr. Mazankowski's first budget. There we read:

"The Co-operative Housing Program will be terminated immediately."

At page 67 of the Mulroney team's *Handbook* we find the following promise:

"To support the rights, liberties and freedoms of Canadians, a P.C. Government is committed to assisting Charter of Rights cases deemed of national importance."

This assistance, of course, is provided through the Court Challenges Program. In February, 1990, funding for the program was terminated and all staff were informed that they no longer had jobs. In response to public protest, the government relented, and in May of that year, the Mulroney team announced that the Court Challenges Program was being extended for five years. Apparently no one on the team can count past two, because in February 1992, funding was again terminated, and this time, for good.

So we had a promise. It was broken. A new promise was made. It too was broken. At least there is consistency. If as a member of the Mulroney party, you make a promise, consistency requires that you break that promise.

Was the Minister of Justice and Attorney General of Canada ashamed or even uncomfortable with what was being done to the Court Challenges Program? The answer is No. Ms. Campbell lectured the members of the House of Commons as follows:

"One of the axioms one learns in public life is that there is no limit to the amount of good you can do, but there may be a limit to the amount of good you can afford." (*Hansard*, Feb. 28/92, p. 7767)

Think of all the wonderful good things she could do if only there was the money. Never mind that the lack of money ceased to be a problem when it came to things like the Mulroney "Farewell to Europe" tour. Later that same day, on the same issue, Ms. Campbell said:

"It may be that from time to time it will be appropriate to take the litigation response and at that time we would look at the appropriate nature of funding." (p. 7769)

Her mentor could hardly have said it better himself; he is a great teacher. So much for the Court Challenges Program. But enough of broken promises in the *PC Campaign Handbook*.

"YOU HAD AN OPTION"

Remembering our underlying theme — promise versus performance — we have seen Mr. Mulroney spouting promises from the very first day he decided to run for the leadership of the Conservative Party. Promise-making continued non-stop throughout the next year, and with the election call, reached a fever pitch.

Canadians, of course, wondered how much all those promises would cost. At that time, they naïvely thought that Mr. Mulroney and his team took their promises seriously, so the question was a legitimate one. It became even more relevant with the accidental disclosure of the Mulroney team's own estimate of the billions of dollars at stake. Very early in the campaign, an *Ottawa Citizen* reporter observed that a document being carried by Conservative finance critic John Crosbie estimated that promises made a week earlier by Mr. Mulroney while in Prince Albert Saskatchewan would cost between $5.5 billion and $6.6 billion over five years.

The *Ottawa Citizen* of July 11, 1984, reported:

If the party goes ahead and unveils "all the programs we have committed ourselves to," the bill will leap to more than $20 billion, the document says.

The document expresses concern about how the programs would be financed, but the part seen by the reporter did not outline options in that area.

What did Mulroney think about his finance critic's calculations? The article continues:

Mulroney appeared stunned when asked by a reporter if he thought the $6.6-billion pricetag on the Prince Albert proposals was excessive.

"Why? Are you...is there something that you'd, uh ... uh ... I ... I'm sorry, I don't follow your question," he fumbled.

Later he answered, "I wouldn't comment on it, but clearly it is (excessive) .... The Liberals have been peddling that figure since this morning."

However, Crosbie, when asked later if the paper had been circulated by the Liberals, said: "If you say you saw it and it

was under my arm, then it would be my document.... I had no Liberal papers."

Mulroney could have dispelled all of the anxiety by revealing that the actual cost would be negligible because the promises were not going to be kept. That, however, would not have enhanced his election prospects, so the next day, he gamely defended his orgy of promise-making. The full cost, he said, would be less than $20 billion; but he gave no information about how much less. Whatever the figure, wouldn't this mean increasing the deficit? Instead of pledging to wage war on the deficit, Mr. Mulroney replied:

"Our job creation proposals are set out in a responsible fiscal framework that calls for the full payment in a responsible and proper manner. ...From time to time, certain costs may be involved that will have the offsetting effect of creating wealth." (*Ottawa Citizen*, July 14/84)

Still no preoccupation with the deficit! Economic growth, new government expenditures, and the creation of wealth were the priority during this election campaign. The *PC Campaign Handbook*, at page 97, said, "**We can reduce the deficit without increasing taxes or reducing the level of social services**", and this undoubtedly is what Conservative candidates, like Wilson and Charest, were telling their electorates throughout the country. In the meantime, promises continued to flow like the Mississippi in full spate.

While on a swing through the West, Mr. Mulroney repeated some old promises and then proclaimed:

"I'm not afraid to inflict prosperity on western Canada." (Globe and Mail, July 23/84)

In the Maritimes, he said:

"I have no hesitation in inflicting prosperity on Atlantic Canada." (Chronicle-Herald, Aug. 1/84)

Not only were his words inflated; so also was his ego. The *Globe and Mail* of August 2, 1984, reports how Mr. Mulroney's entourage swept into New Brunswick.

At the Charlo airport, he was greeted by a majorette corps and band that played The Stars and Stripes Forever. At a Chatham shopping mall, it was music again befitting a U.S. presidential campaign, as an organist played Hail to the Chief.

Impressed, Mr. Mulroney remained true to that presidential style to the very end. He always seemed to feel like the President of Canada when standing arm in arm, literally or figuratively, with the President of the United States of America.

But back to promises. In Halifax on August 2, 1984, Mulroney gave a major policy speech on his plans for the Atlantic region. Part of the text reads:

"A Progressive Conservative government will guarantee to maintain — and if necessary enhance — the Maritime Freight Rate Subsidy Assistance Program."

We've heard that promise from him earlier. In a background paper released that same day by the Atlantic Caucus of the Conservative Party, there was the claim:

...the Liberal government continues to attempt to dismantle vital transportation assistance programs such as the maritime Freight Rate Assistance Program and the *"At and East"* rates.

But as we've seen, it was Mr. Mulroney's Conservative government, not the Liberals, who went on to cut back the Maritime Freight Assistance Program and then abolished the "At and East" rates. When they were abolished by Bill C-11, ministers such as Kim Campbell and Jean Charest voted in support of the legislation. Mulroney himself was absent.

In his August 2, 1984 speech, Mr. Mulroney also said:

"A Progressive Conservative government will reinstate VIA Rail routes, including the "Atlantic Limited" from Halifax to Montreal; support and continue to operate the Newfoundland railway (Terra Transport)."

What actually happened was, we now know, quite predictable. No longer is there a railway in Newfoundland. As for *reinstating*

VIA Rail routes, the Conservative team *abandoned* existing routes throughout Atlantic Canada and the rest of the country. In his Halifax speech, Mr. Mulroney also promised:

> "We will examine gasoline, alcohol, food and lodging taxes which are reducing the competitiveness of Canada's tourism industry."

What did he do? He increased the gasoline tax. He increased the tax on alcohol so many times that smuggling has become a major problem. Finally, he introduced the GST and applied it to lodgings and restaurant meals. That's how the Mulroney government helped tourism.

Mulroney's tours through Quebec during the election campaign were particularly interesting. We have already seen how, on Sept. 5, 1983, he said:

> "By their referendum response, Quebecers have put an end to the question of separation. As far as I'm concerned, the debate is closed."

Eleven months later, in Sept-Iles, he reopened the debate with a vengeance.

> "In Quebec — and it is very obvious — there are wounds to be healed, worries to be calmed, enthusiasms to be rekindled and bonds of trust to be established. ...The men and women of this province have undergone a collective trauma." (*Globe and Mail*, Aug. 7/84)

According to Graham Fraser, of the *Globe and Mail*, Mulroney's speech...

> "was a remarkable appeal to nationalist sentiment in Quebec for a man who in the past had been very critical of his predecessor, Joe Clark, for his tolerant attitude toward the Parti Québécois.
>
> The speech was full of codewords aimed at those who voted for the PQ in 1981, and who were angry at the way Quebec was left out of the constitutional settlement the same year."

Later that month, Mr. Mulroney charged: **"the Liberal Party of having 'a well articulated and well defined' policy to 'brutalize the Government of Quebec'."** (*Globe and Mail,* Aug. 20/84)

Throughout the remainder of the campaign, Premier Rene Levesque had only nice things to say about Mr. Mulroney, and his separatist supporters flocked to Mulroney's side. The rest, as they say, is history. Sad history!

In Ontario, Mr. Mulroney promised not only to safeguard existing social programs, but to create new ones.

> **"No longer can child care be considered a luxury of the rich or a support program for the poor,"** he said. **"It is an urgent problem for thousands of single-parent families and a major concern in every family where both parents work."**

> **Mulroney said child care would be a priority of a Conservative government because it would free more people to work or upgrade their skills. "It must become an integral part of the workplace. ...*Urgency* here is of paramount concern."** (***London Free Press,*** **Aug. 11/84)**

What has been done in the intervening nine years to address this "urgent" problem? Not much. There is no national program for child care. In fact, the Mulroney team actually has cut back on Canada Assistance Plan funding, a Liberal government program which helps provinces create new child care spaces. So this was a commitment that was broken with a vengeance.

The same newspaper article also describes Mulroney's standard promise of **"a massive training effort",** and describes how, almost without exception, the Conservative leader was greeted warmly wherever he went. The one exception was Alex Belanger, a technician in the Electrohome plant in Kitchener, who remarked: **"Conservative snake who slithers through the earth".** Apparently, Mr. Mulroney was not fooling everyone.

In Kingston, Mr. Mulroney promised to lift the lid off government secrecy, particularly where salaries were concerned.

> **"For all these highly placed public servants, a counter-democratic principle has been long enforced. It is that, while**

the Government has a responsibility to pay their salaries, the public has no right to know how much they are paying."

The public should have the right "to know the salaries of all public officials, no matter how exalted," he said. (*Globe and Mail*, Aug. 13/84)

We can add this to the list of unkept promises.

Mr. Mulroney also promised changes to the personal income tax system.

"Our goal is to ensure that wealthy Canadians with substantial unearned income cannot use tax shelters to avoid paying tax altogether — that they must pay a minimum amount of tax," he said. (*Toronto Star*, August 25/84)

The same article also describes how Mulroney told reporters **"that a Tory government would require rich people to pay a 'handsome amount' of tax."** The only people who paid "handsome" amounts of tax under the Mulroney administration were the poor and middle class. In fact, they paid more than handsome amounts, even new taxes on vitamins and aspirin and bandages for their children. What about the wealthy? "We'll get back to them", to use an early Mulroney phrasing, to find out about the treatment they received. Handsome it was; most handsome!

The general election of 1984 racked up a very long list of promises. Promises of jobs, jobs, jobs, of doubling research and development expenditures, of new training programs and of the sanctity of our universal social programs. As we've seen, we would not be exaggerating too much if we said that whenever a promise was made by Mr. Mulroney and his gang during the campaign, the result was a promise broken by his administration. With characteristic insincerity, while vowing to keep their promises, they charged that Canada's other parties couldn't be relied on to keep theirs. The *PC Campaign Handbook* states:

The Liberals do not believe in honesty and openness in government, no matter what they say.

In contrast, we have this high statement of principle about Mr. Mulroney's party.

> **The Progressive Conservative party is proposing policies and a new style of government that can realize Canada's great potential. Our promises will be kept because they are realistic and genuine, and because we will work with all Canadians to fulfil them.**

Canadians now have Ms. Campbell, a loyal and zealous supporter of Mulroney, trying to convince Canadians that that is exactly what happened between 1984 and 1993, and that her promises are equally "realistic and genuine." If they are "equally" realistic and genuine, then we know they are neither. Past performance shows they will be unrealistic and hypocritical. The principle of "contrary performance" has never been abandoned by the Conservative party as reconstituted by Mulroney.

Let's end this chapter with the personal vision Mr. Mulroney shared with reporters while waiting for the election call.

> **"What is going to happen is that there is going to be an election campaign, and we're going to drive this government from office. And you're going to have millions of people cheering on the sidelines, including people who've got investments bottled up. As soon as Knowlton Nash comes on television saying that the Tories have formed a majority government, investment is going to flow into this country....**
>
> **"The mere fact of the election of a PC majority government committed to the principles I've been talking about will create a hallelujah chorus around the world...."** (*Whig Standard*, Sept. 8/84)

Mr. Mulroney won the 1984 general election, but there was no "hallelujah chorus around the world", except, perhaps, in some corporate boardrooms south of the border and elsewhere. Those hallelujah choruses would be justifiably loud, and while not challenging Handel in artistry, would rival his famous chorus in volume.

As for the millions of cheering Canadians in Mr. Mulroney's vision, they weren't there. What was there — to switch from Handel to Dickens — were the great expectations of a people soon to suffer the disillusion and pain of promises cynically made and ruthlessly broken.

6.

NOW THAT WE'RE ELECTED, WHAT DO WE DO ABOUT OUR PROMISES, PARTICULARLY ON R&D?

WE NOW PASS OVER A DIVIDE, leaving behind the *promises* of *candidate* Mulroney and his party and coming to the *performance* of *Prime Minister* Mulroney and the Conservative government. Actually, his performance as Prime Minister began with more promises. But that is for later. Let us set the scene by recalling the wise and enlightened words of candidate Mulroney. Those are important words for all those Canadians who want to assign responsibility for the current mess.

As the 1984 general election campaign began, Mr. Mulroney declared:

> "The government was not one man, not even a prime minister, and neither its record nor its accountability retired with him.
>
> Most Liberal candidates in this election were an integral part of that record as ministers and MPs who proposed it and approved it and now they must answer to the people of Canada for it." (*Ottawa Citizen*, July 10/84)

If we apply these words to 1993, Mr. Mulroney would say:

> "The government is not one man, not even the prime minister, and neither its record nor its accountability retired with <u>me</u>.
>
> All <u>Conservative</u> candidates in the recent leadership race were an integral part of that record as ministers and MP's who proposed it and approved it and now they must answer to the people of Canada for it."

Who were these candidates? We had two ministers — Kim Campbell and Jean Charest — who sat at the cabinet table manufacturing the policies that have caused such hardship to Canadians. They now sit as Prime Minister and Deputy-Prime Minister. As the editorial page of the June 7 issue of *Maclean's* magazine observes, the **"front-runners are partners in the same cabinet, responsible for the same legacy."**

Campbell and Charest were not out on the fringe. Both sat on the powerful Cabinet Committee on Priorities and Planning, which is chaired by the Prime Minister himself. They, hands on, established and set the priorities and policy goals of their government — priorities such as the GST and Free Trade and NAFTA.

Mr. Charest was chosen by Mulroney to be Vice-Chairman of the Cabinet Committee on Communications. This Committee was in charge of government propaganda — which we now know is usually disinformation. It decided how and where to spend millions of government advertising dollars, in an attempt to dissuade Canadians from what they know — that Tory times are bad.

According to Conservative MP Patrick Boyer, both Campbell and Charest are protégés of Mr. Mulroney. In a CBC Radio interview, aired on May 11, 1993, Mr. Boyer said:

"Well it's a case of both Jean Charest and Kim Campbell, each of whom is a protégé of Prime Minister Mulroney. He brought them in and gave them the advantages and promoted them...."

Mr. Mulroney did more than promote them. In the case of Jean Charest, there was a resurrection. When Charest was forced to resign from cabinet following a telephone call to a judge, Mr. Mulroney carefully nursed him back.

In Ms. Campbell, we had a minister who complained that Canadians misunderstand and fail to appreciate the true grandeur of Mr. Mulroney. She says:

"He [Mulroney] always comes down on the right side of an issue.... I have enormous respect for his competence...." (*Globe and Mail*, May 20/93)

If Ms. Campbell is right, then most Canadians are wrong. Ms. Campbell was also quoted in the *Toronto Star* of October 30, 1992 as saying of Mr. Mulroney:

"Every time I go somewhere with the Prime Minister, I see *warmth*, I see great *respect*..."

What of the other three leadership candidates — Jim Edwards, Patrick Boyer, and Garth Turner? Edwards and Boyer were first elected to the House of Commons in 1984 and both served as Parliamentary Secretaries. All three voted for Mulroney's legislation. They, along with other Conservatives, furnished the votes needed to pass the FTA, the GST, the NAFTA, and to dismantle our social programs.

Jim Edwards was appointed President of the Treasury Board by Prime Minister Campbell on June 25th of this year. Ms. Campbell must have been impressed when she heard him say, **"I would have the GST apply to every transaction that exists"**, including groceries. (*CBC Morningside,* May 24/93)

The record we are examining is the record of these five individuals and their colleagues. To quote Mr. Mulroney himself, **"They were an integral part of that record — as ministers and MPs who proposed it and approved it — and now they must answer to the people of Canada for it."** What is it they have to answer for?

The Speech from the Throne of November 5, 1984, would be a reasonable place to start, but we do not find much there. The Speech repeated some earlier promises, studiously ignored others, and confidently proclaimed:

> **"This is the inauguration of a new Parliament. Let it be also the beginning of a new era of national reconciliation, economic renewal and social justice. In this spirit, my Ministers will honour the mandate entrusted to them by the people of Canada."**

Did those ministers honour their mandate? Did the Mulroney administration achieve "national reconciliation"? Did the Mulroney team give Canadians "economic renewal"? Did the Mulroney gang provide "social justice"? They did not. But now they want Canadians to invite them back for more. Let's begin with Finance Minister Michael Wilson's Economic Statement of November 8, 1984. The first challenge the new Minister of Finance set for the Mulroney team was:

"**to put our own fiscal house in order so that we can limit, and ultimately reverse, the massive build-up in public debt and the damaging impact this has on confidence and growth**".

We did not hear much about the deficit during the election campaign, but now it was the priority. What was the fiscal situation late in 1984? What was the deficit? After two months of scouring over the books, Mr. Wilson had the answer. He told the members of the House of Commons that with **"no policy changes, the deficit for this fiscal year [1984-85] would be $34.5 billion...."** Mr. Wilson then said **"This is what we inherited."** Those words can be found on page 4 of Wilson's *Financial Statement*.

The new finance minister then announced some policy changes which he calculated would raise the deficit to $34.577 billion. That's at page 16 of his *Economic Statement*. His calculator must have been defective because by the end of the 1984-85 fiscal year, the deficit had increased not by $77 million, but by virtually $4 billion, to $38.4 billion. Not a very auspicious start for the new minister! If he had done nothing and simply sat in his office twiddling his thumbs, the deficit would have been $34.5 billion. That's what he said he had inherited from the Liberals. That's what he said the deficit would be if he did nothing — $34.5 billion. Instead, he did something and the deficit shot up to $38.4 billion.

What exactly did he do? This is where the story gets interesting. One of the things he did was juggle government expenditures. Some programs and departments got more money, and some got less.

Who got less?

Well, among the unlucky branches of government were those engaged in research and development, and scientific pursuits. They got less. Readers will say that cannot be true. In previous chapters we saw Mr. Mulroney preach about the importance of R&D and about how he would double expenditures on R&D as a percentage of Gross Domestic Product. He preached about R&D while a businessman. He made promises about doubling R&D while a candidate for his party's leadership. He even devoted an entire chapter to the subject in his book, *Where I Stand*. He preached and made more promises while a Member of Parliament. He preached and promised throughout the 1984 general election campaign. But when finally given an opportunity, after years and years of complaining, promising and preaching, what did he do?

The answer is contained in the report the President of the Treasury Board, Robert de Cotret, presented to the House of Commons, in November 1984. The document is entitled *"Expenditure and Program Review"* and contains an appendix of programs to be cut or eliminated. Here are some of the targetted programs:

Cuts of $4.4 million by discontinuing research programs into x-rays, Nuclear Radiation and High Presure chemistry.

Cuts of $5 million to the research facilities of the Environment Secretariat.

Cuts of $23 million by cancelling construction of the proposed Manufacturing Technology Institute in Winnipeg.

Cuts of $3.6 million by cancelling the proposed Institute for Electrochemistry and the Cold Regions Research Institute.

Cuts of $4.9 million by deferring construction of a pharmaceutical testing laboratory and a plant health laboratory.

Mr. de Cotret's report states:

Longer term or lower priority research work will be curtailed in the following departments and agencies:

	($ millions)
Agriculture	2.7
Canada Mortgage and Housing Corporation	0.2
Consumer and Corporate Affairs	0.7
Energy Mines and Resources1	4.4
Environment	2.8
Forestry	1.4
Fisheries and Oceans	1.5
National Research Council	34.6
Public Works	0.6
Transport	1.9
TOTAL	60.8

More than $60 million in cuts, including $34.6 million to the National Research Council. In his book *Where I Stand*, Mr. Mulroney said:

"The National Research Council, which acts as Canada's main research laboratory, needs a funding increase of at least 20 per cent...." (p. 40)

That was what the NRC needed. What did Mulroney give it? — a $34.6 million cut in funding.

Research and Development programs were among the very first programs the new Mulroney team slashed. They were slashed within 2 months of the Tories taking office. Research and Development had been assigned absolutely the lowest priority. Instead of going back to Michael Wilson's *Economic Statement*, let's break away from our chronology and continue with the R&D story. Remember, that for Mr. Mulroney, research and development represented the lifeblood of an industrial nation.

Speaking at the University of Toronto, on March 14, 1984, Mr. Mulroney had said:

"...we are spending 1.3 per cent of GNP on research and development. As the principal of McGill University has stated, 'we are writing a suicide note for our competitive capacities in the 1990s'."

On March 22, in Montreal, Mr. Mulroney vowed:

"We're going to double our collective national commitment to research and development within the life of our first government mandate."

Both these quotations are from the PC election paper: *On the Issues; Brian Mulroney and the Progressive Conservative Agenda — Statements of Policy and Principle, July 1984*, at page 15.

According to Statistics Canada publication, *Science Statistics, Vol. 16, No. 3*, the portion of GDP devoted to research and development in 1976 was 1.03 per cent. By 1984, under Liberal government policies, it had risen to 1.37 per cent. This is what Mr. Mulroney inherited, what he characterized as a "suicide note" for the future, and what he promised to double by the end of his first mandate.

In 1988, at the end of Mulroney's first mandate, the percentage of the GDP devoted to research and development was no longer 1.37 per cent — it was 1.36 per cent. That's how the Mulroney team doubled R&D expenditures during its first term. As we approach the end of the second mandate, can we now say that expenditures have doubled? The answer is No. In 1991, the percentage of GDP devoted to research and development was 1.43 per cent. So over seven years, the Mulroney team just barely managed an increase — an increase of 0.06 points.

According to Statistics Canada, we are behind France, we are behind Germany, we are behind Japan, we are behind Sweden, we are behind the U.K., we are behind the U.S., and we are on the verge of being overtaken by Italy, over which we had a substantial lead in 1984 when Mr. Mulroney and his team talked about increasing and doubling R&D. Statistics Canada reports that our R&D/GDP ratio is **"lower than that of most industrialized OECD countries."** It also states: **"The federal government has become relatively less involved in both funding and performance of R&D...."**

How is it that Canada is falling behind, particularly in light of the endless promises made by Mr. Mulroney and his colleagues in 1984? A Review of the newspaper articles on the subject since the Mulroney team took over will quickly reveal the answer. Let's do that now, but instead of reviewing the entire last eight years, let's use 1986 as an example of how R&D has been nurtured by the Mulroney team. Some of the newspaper headlines of that year read:

"Budget said blow to councils which fund scientific research";

"Government figures for research funding paint grim picture for university scientists";

"Government stalled on science spending goals";

"Ill effect of research cuts predicted soon";

"Canada lags far behind in R&D spending";

"Govt. chops research fund by $30 million";

"Cut in R&D support angers high-tech group";

"What's happened to Brian's lofty high-tech vows?";

NOW THAT WE'RE ELECTED...

"More cuts in R&D";

"PM's research crusade evaporates";

"Research groups 'fearing the knife' ";

"Le budget du Conseil national de la rechcerche réduit de $20 millions";

"NRC budget axe fells world famous scientist";

"Federal cuts to research council end section that spawned winner".

That last article, from the *Globe and Mail* of October 16, reads in part:

The National Research Council plans to scrap its photochemistry and kinetics section — where John Polanyi, Canada's newest Novel Prize winner, started his pioneering research.... "It is an unfortunate coincidence," Dr. Ross Pottie, NRC senior vice-president of laboratories, said in an interview later. "We had no idea Dr. Polanyi was going to win the Noble Prize today." ...Among the research programs and personnel also affected by the cuts announced by Dr. Kerwin yesterday — only two weeks after the Conservatives pledged in the throne speech to stimulate technological development — are electromagnetic and mechanical engineering, environmental toxicology, aeronautics, construction and physics.

Other headlines read:

"Research cuts shame Mulroney";

"Save research group Canadian chemists urge prime minister";

"100 to 150 will lose NRC jobs, offical says";

"Draft R&D plans ask Ottawa to cut thousands of jobs".

An article in the *Ottawa Citizen*, of October 31, 1906, entitled, "Canada will become third-rate if cuts continue, say scientists" reads:

—73—

"Canada will be reduced to a third-rate developing country providing raw materials instead of technology ... One scientific researcher said it seems the government is bent on destroying the country's mind while snuffing out its soul through similar cuts in support of the arts."

Other articles are headlined as follows:

"Leaked NRC memo says observatory forced to shut down because of cuts";

"NRC appeals to Ottawa to save cancer program";

"NRC axes renowned 'Canadian' scientist".

That last headline is from the *Ottawa Citizen*, of November 6, and the article begins:

"A National Research Council scientist, whose work on the U.S. space shuttle's robotic Canadarm was recently commemorated on a Canadian stamp, has been axed in the latest round of NRC cuts."

More headlines: "**Mulroney policy devastating scientific research**" and "**Basic research is put in jeopardy by Ottawa's cuts.**"

Finally, one last entry, this one from the *Toronto Star*, of December 14, 1986. "**More cuts ahead for research council science minister says**". But it was not all bad news. Another story, in the same newspaper, on the same day, on the very same page, is headed: "**Ottawa gives underwear firm $800,000 deal**". Unfortunately for the Mulroneyites, there are no Nobel Prize winners in the field of underwear.

When Canada's international R&D position began to slip, whose fault was it? According to Mr. Mulroney, fault did not lie with the Mulroney Conservatives. Nothing is ever their fault — that's another principle. An article appearing in the *Ottawa Sun* of June 20, 1989, carries the headline:

"**R&D MUST INCREASE: PM**".

The first paragraph reads:

"Prime Minister Brian Mulroney blamed business and high schools last night for Canada's poor research and development record."

That's who was to blame!

What were the members of the Mulroney team doing while all this slashing was going on? Nothing. As Mr. Mulroney said in 1984, they **"were an integral part of that record as ministers and MP's who proposed it and approved it and now they must answer to the people of Canada for it."** But instead of answering to the people of Canada, they are doing more of the same in 1993.

Canadian scientists are fearing a renewed brain drain after the federal government reneged on a promise to increase research money by 4 per cent a year for the next four years.

They're also alarmed by reports that Ottawa plans to slash financing for its 15 Centres of Excellence, which do applied research in such fields as pesticides, aging, robotics and genetics.

"We're going to have a brain drain crisis that you wouldn't believe" **if the government carries through on its plans, said Howard Dickson, chairman of the newly formed Coalition for Biomedical and Health Research.** (*Toronto Star*, Apr. 30/93)

The *Ottawa Citizen* of May 7, 1993 reports:

Funding for the federal government's flagship science program may be cut even though the program is considered a success says Science Minister Tom Hockin.

Hockin says he doubts he can convince cabinet that funding for the National Networks of Centres of Excellence should be maintained at the current level.

When Mr. Hockin was moved out of the Science portfolio in late June, 1993, he still had not been able to convince his cabinet colleagues and Prime Minister Kim Campbell not to slash the spending.

While campaigning for the leadership of her party, Ms. Campbell, of course, said all the right things about R&D. On May 12, 1993, in a press release, she said:

"I am committed to a science and technology strategy that will support the growth of high tech companies and the creation of well paying jobs for Canadians".

We all know how she helped Mr. Mulroney keep similar promises while in his cabinet. Three days after Ms. Campbell was sworn-in as Canada's new prime minister, more R&D cuts were announced.

The federal government is dismantling another of its science bodies, the second in a year.

The Department of External Affairs is winding up its science and technology division, a move it says will streamline trade in high-tech businesses.

But the division's deputy director, Victor Bradley, said the closing will deprive Canada of chances to take part in international research and development. (Ottawa Citizen, June 28/93)

Campbell's next target was the National Network of Centres of Excellence. On August 3, 1993, her Science Minister, Rob Nicholson, announced that funding for this R&D program would be slashed by $115 million over four years. (*Ottawa Citizen*, Aug. 4/93)

Prime Minister Campbell, following in the footsteps of her mentor, Brian Mulroney, has wasted no time in showing where her priorities lie.

So there we have the story of Canadian research and development under Mulroney and Campbell. Mr. Mulroney says, **"We kept our word."**

7.

MICHAEL WILSON, THE ONE TRILLION DOLLAR MAN

MR. WILSON'S LEGACY AS FINANCE MINISTER is important not only because of the misery it has left throughout Canada, but because it is a legacy that Prime Minister Campbell has adopted as her own. When leadership candidate Kim Campbell presented her economic policy proposals on April 29, 1993, she began by praising Mr. Mazankowski's most recent budget and then said:

> "**I am totally supportive of the Government's economic direction first laid out by Michael Wilson and consistently followed since then.**"

As for the government's economic and fiscal record, she said: "**I am proud of that record.**" Then she crowed that she had "**sat on the Expenditure Review Committee of Cabinet.**" (Press Release)

She was proud of Michael Wilson's record, and, as we learned, Michael Wilson was proud of her. Less than two weeks following Campbell's pledge of allegiance to his policies, Wilson announced he was supporting Campbell's leadership bid. He had a good reason:

> "**I think she is very much committed to the (economic) policies that I have been very much a part of in recent years.**" (*Toronto Star*, May 11/93)

Canadians are entitled to ask: "What are those policies Mr. Wilson is talking about, those policies to which Ms. Campbell is committed, and what have they accomplished for Canada." Let's begin with the big picture.

Under the guidance of Finance Minister Michael Wilson, and later Don Mazankowski, the Mulroney Conservatives in 8 years accomplished what all previous Prime Ministers and Finance Ministers combined could not accomplish in 117 years. They spent more than one trillion dollars!

THE SHOW MUST NOT GO ON

Seventeen Prime Ministers, from Macdonald to Turner, governing since Confederation, spent $900 billion over 117 years. Then along came Mulroney, who, with the help of Wilson, Mazankowski, Campbell, Charest and friends, managed to spend more than one trillion dollars in 8 years. It is hard to believe that a government trying to pass itself off as frugal and fiscally responsible and Conservative, could spend so much.

The Mulroney government was elected in September of 1984. Though Finance Minister Michael Wilson presented his economic statement in November 1984, let's pretend that the Mulroney team did not spend a single penny until the new year — January 1, 1985. We will give Mr. Wilson a 4-month period of grace.

Between January 1, 1985 and March 31, 1985 — the final quarter of the 1984-85 fiscal year — the new government spent approximately $27 billion. In the 1985-86 fiscal year, the Mulroney team spent $111 billion.

In 1986-87—$116 billion
In 1987-88—$125 billion
In 1988-89—$132 billion
In 1989-90—$143 billion
In 1990-91—$151 billion
In 1991-92—$155 billion
In 1992-93—$158 billion

For the first quarter of the 1993-94 fiscal year, which takes us to the end of June 1993, the Mulroney Conservatives spent another $40 billion, for a grand total of one trillion, one hundred and fifty eight billion dollars.

One trillion dollars, is a staggering figure that can be appreciated only when put into a more graspable perspective. If you spent one million dollars a day, it would take 2,739 years to spend a trillion dollars — the Mulroneyites spent it in 8 years. One trillion dollars would build new $100,000 homes for ten million Canadian families. You could give every man, woman and child living in Canada almost $40,000.

What did Canadians get for the one trillion one hundred and fifty eight billion dollars of their money that the Mulroneyites spent? Not much. They got record numbers of unemployed, the dismantling of their social programs, and a colossal national debt for their children. But in 1984, it wasn't supposed to turn out like this. In his November 1984 *Economic Statement*, Mr. Wilson explained how terrible things were and then warned:

> **"That is bad enough but that is not the worst of it. Current projections show the deficit .... remaining between $34 and $38 billion in every year for the rest of this decade."** (p. 4)

That's what would happen if he did not act. And what was Mr. Mazankowski's deficit last year? It was $35.5 billion. In order to defend their own dismal performance, Mulroney and Mazankowski claim that Mr. Wilson didn't know what he was talking about in 1984. In a speech Mr. Mazankowski gave to the Vancouver Board of Trade on September 9, 1991, he said:

> **"...if we had not taken action to bring down the rate of spending from its pace prior to 1984-85, the deficit today would be over $100 billion..."**

Mr. Mulroney has himself been spouting identical nonsense on television, evidently not caring that it makes Mr. Wilson appear grossly incompetent.

In his 1984 *Economic Statement*, Mr. Wilson announced that if nothing was done to change the direction of government, **"by 1990 it [the net federal debt] could approach $410 billion."** Today, the net federal debt is approximately $460 billion. Does this mean that Mr. Wilson now admits that less than nothing was done? No he doesn't. He and the other members of the team pull new numbers out of thin air, saying anything, so long as it makes people forget what he said in 1984.

Will Canadians forget how Mr. Wilson said that if nothing were done, **"unemployment would remain unacceptably high — 11 per cent through 1985 and then declining gradually to about 7 per cent by 1990."**? That's at page 4 of his *Economic Statement*. That's the terrible fate Mr. Wilson warned would befall Canadians had the Liberals had been left in charge. Well, the Mulroneyites took over, and by the end of 1990 the unemployment rate was 9.5%. Today, it is over 11%. Clearly, Mr. Wilson and his fellow Mulroneyites not only failed to achieve their own goals, but also failed to attain even the kind of performance they warned would take place under a Liberal government. And Prime Minister Campbell says "job well done," and vows to stay the course.

Mr. Wilson's 1984 *Economic Statement* illustrates how the Tory train went off the tracks even before it had cleared the station. It's time, however, to move on. Let's move directly to Mr. Michael Wilson's first Budget, presented on May 23, 1985.

Eight months after the election, one would have hoped that the members of the Mulroney team finally had a handle on what they were doing. Mr. Wilson would prove otherwise. Let's begin by determining what the minister thought about the state of the economy when he took over:

> "In Canada, our economy grew strongly in 1984. Real growth was 4.7 per cent, the highest since 1976. Inflation averaged 4.4. per cent, the lowest since 1971. Inflation has since fallen below 4 per cent." (Budget Speech, p. 3)

This was the Liberal legacy, but in retrospect, Mr. Wilson was too candid, because the Mulroneyites are now scrambling to rewrite history. Documents from the Department of Finance now claim:

> "In 1984 the country was at an economic crossroads... Real growth had slowed and inflation and unemployment had risen." (*Charting the Economic Course*, April 1993, p. 2)

Once again, who cares if the statement is false, and that it contradicts the words uttered by Finance Minister Michael Wilson in 1985. The important thing is to salvage the situation today, whatever the cost.

Let's continue with Mr. Wilson's 1985 budget. Therein, he declared:

> "I am implementing a clear and realistic medium term plan to control our debt." (p. 5)

What is the result of that "clear and realistic" plan? The result is a debt that has more than doubled since the Mulroney team bought into the plan. Furthermore, that spectacular failure occurred concurrently with spectacular tax increases and determined assaults on our social programs. We all remember Mr. Wilson's declaration in the House of Commons on March 6, 1984: **"We would not raise taxes."** We all remember the 1984 *PC Campaign Handbook*, which said, at page 97: **"We can reduce the deficit without increasing taxes or reducing the level of social services."** Clearly, Mr. Wilson hadn't been listening to what he himself had been saying, or reading what his party had been writing, because on May 23, 1985, he did both. He increased taxes and launched the first of his many assaults on our social services.

Let us start with taxes. First, there was "a temporary 18-month surtax" on personal incomes. Eight years later, Canadians are still waiting to see the end of that 18-month temporary tax. The temporary surtax was to apply to "high-income earners." By "high-income", the Mulroney team meant a family of 4 with an income of $40,000. That is where the surtax would kick-in.

The second tax increase introduced by Mr. Wilson was not, strictly speaking, a tax increase, but it would raise even more money than the surtax. Personal tax exemptions, such as the married exemption, no longer would increase with the cost of living. They would be deindexed, increasing only by the amount that inflation exceeded 3 per cent. Therefore, if inflation were 4%, the personal exemptions would increase by only one per cent. This would take place year after year, and the value of the exemptions would become smaller year after year. In the 1986 calendar year, this change alone would raise $635 million in extra taxes from Canadians, and in years following, it would raise billions.

Page 74 of the *Budget Papers* shows that this deindexation of personal exemptions would cost a family of 4, earning a meagre $15,000 annually, an extra $62 in taxes. These lower income families also lost the benefit of the Federal Tax Reduction provision. This meant another $100 in taxes for our family of 4 with an annual income of $15,000.

Next, there was an increase in the Federal Sales Tax rate. Immediately upon taking office, the Mulroney team increased the tax from 9% to 10%, effective October 1, 1984. In his 1985 budget, Wilson increased it again, to 11%. This was the same tax he was later to characterize as the "silent killer of jobs" when trying to convince Canadians that the GST would be good for them. The scope of this "silent-killer-of-jobs" sales tax was also expanded. It would now apply to confectioneries, soft drinks, pet foods, energy conservation products, and health products such as medicated creams, bandages, surgical and dental instruments.

Then the excise tax on tobacco was increased. The excise tax on alcohol was increased. Excise taxes on transportation fuels were increased. There were special new taxes on corporations and financial institutions. This was quite a start for someone who said **"We would not raise taxes."** And he wasn't finished!

The Registered Home Ownership Savings Plan, which assisted young families to save money for their first homes, was abolished. Turning to social programs, Mr. Wilson proposed to deindex old age security payments, so that there would be no annual increases unless inflation exceeded 3 per cent. The Mulroney team abandoned that proposal when seniors across the country rightly charged that they had been betrayed. However, identical proposal to deindex family allowances become law.

The children of Canada were a softer touch for the Mulroney team — they were a safer target, seeing how they were much less likely to demonstrate on Parliament Hill. So Mr. Wilson also announced that, starting in 1987 income tax exemptions for children, which stood at $710 per child, would not merely be deindexed, but that they would be reduced, first to $560, and then to $470. As we all know, for the 1993 taxation year, they have been eliminated altogether. As if that weren't enough, the income threshold for the child tax credit would be reduced by $3,000, and the exemption for dependent children over the age of 18 would be reduced.

Were all these new taxes and cuts to social programs designed to cut the deficit? With their implementation, did the Mulroney team get a firm handle on the deficit? The answer to both questions is No, because unfortunately, all the savings and all the new taxes, paid even by the very poorest of Canadians, did not go to fighting the deficit. A large part was redirected for the benefit of Canadians who least needed the government's help. In particular, we are referring to changes Mr. Wilson made to capital gains and RRSPs.

Let us deal with capital gains first. In his 1985 budget, Mr. Wilson announced that individuals would be granted a lifetime capital gains exemption of half-a-million dollars. All capital property would qualify for the exemption, whether it was a villa in Bermuda or a vacant lot in downtown Toronto. At page 6 of his budget speech, Mr. Wilson declared:

> **"This is a measure designed to unleash the full entrepreneurial dynamism of individual Canadians."**

Who, exactly, were these individual Canadians whose "entrepreneurial dynamism" was going to be unleashed?

Well, they certainly weren't members of those families of 4 struggling to raise their families on $15,000. They would see their taxes increase now that they had been harnessed to the tax wheel in order to provide the money needed to unleash the dynamism of others. Who were these others?

The answer is provided in the Revenue Canada publication *"Taxation Statistics"*, at page 287. For the 1990 taxation year, capital gains deductions totalled more than $6 billion. Who claimed these deductions? The Revenue Canada publication shows that individuals with an annual income of $80,000 or higher claimed more than $4 billion of those capital gains deductions. That is where the money went. The money that was taken from the middle class and poor through the front door was shovelled out the back door to rich people, at least to people who look rich to those from whom the money was taken. Those are the ones whom the Mulroneyites were determined to help.

This gift to the few, paid for by the many, was going to cost big money, not just peanuts. On page 19 of the 1985 *Fiscal Plan*, there is a chart showing that in the 1985-86 fiscal year, the capital gains exemption was projected to cost the treasury $300 million. This was $80 million <u>more</u> than the government was going to receive through deindexation, the surtax and the elimination of the federal tax reduction, all <u>combined</u>!!

In 1985, Mr. Wilson, despite his tough talk, wasn't increasing taxes on the lower and middle classes to fight the deficit. He was increasing their taxes because he needed the money in order to provide a capital gains windfall for the wealthiest Canadians. It would cost $300 million in the 1985-86 fiscal year, and the following year, it would cost $600 million dollars while it was still being phased in. How many billions of dollars has it cost the federal treasury since then?

The other gift to the wealthy unveiled by Mr. Wilson in 1985 was increased contribution limits for Registered Retirement Savings Plans. Before the Mulroney team came into power, Canadians could put up to $5,500 into an RRSP. These contributions are tax deductible and they may grow within the RRSP tax free. In his budget, Mr. Wilson announced that contribution limits would be raised, in phases, to $15,500, or 18% of earnings, whichever was greater. What individuals did Mr. Wilson think could afford to plunk $15,500 into an RRSP every year? He could not have been thinking about that family of four with an annual income of only $15,000. For those families, Mr. Wilson deindexed personal exemptions, eliminated the Federal Tax Reduction, increased excise taxes, increased sales taxes, and slapped the sales tax onto previously exempt products such as snack foods and bandages. Clearly, he was not thinking of them!

To contribute $15,500, keeping in mind the overall limit of 18% of total income, you would need annual earnings of more than $85,000. That is who Mr. Wilson and Mr. Mulroney were worried about: individuals making more than $85,000 a year. They needed help. Their welfare was more important than the welfare of middle class families struggling to raise their children. It was more important than the deficit. The top priority was to allow these high income individuals to hide an extra $10,000 from the tax-man, while asking all other Canadians to empty their pockets. Though this change was phased in more slowly than Mr. Wilson originally wanted, how many billions of dollars has it cost the treasury since 1985?

So that is the story of Mr. Wilson's first budget. There were new taxes for all Canadians, allegedly to fight the deficit, and boxes of bonbons for the wealthiest Canadians, so that they would be well-nourished when it came time to unleash their dynamism.

What was the net effect? Page 19 of Michael Wilson's 1985 *Fiscal Plan* shows for the 1986-87 fiscal year, sales and excise tax increases of $1.38 billion dollars; personal income tax increases of

$1.6 billion; a $600 million capital gains present to the wealthy; a $40 million RRSP present to the wealthy; and a reduction in corporate taxes of $540 million.

And the final result? For the 1985-86 fiscal year, the result was $34.4 billion deficit.

This then is how the Mulroney team launched Mr. Wilson's **"clear and realistic medium term plan."** It was certainly a fulfilment of a Conservative government's classic role of redistributing the wealth of a nation — redistributing it by taking away from the poor and giving to the rich, like Robin Hood in reverse. It was a plan that kept Mulroney's and Wilson's Bay and Wall Street friends happy. And now those same well-nourished friends say that the deficit is proof that all other Canadians are eating too much and demand that the Tory team work even harder to dismantle what is left of Canada's social programs. Kim Campbell asks: "When can I start?"

There is one additional item from Michael Wilson's 1985 budget that needs to be tied off before we proceed with other matters. We have seen how Mr. Mulroney, while on his promise making binge during the Central Nova by-election campaign, vowed to retain the heavy water plants in Cape Breton until he could attract new industry into the region, possibly high tech industry.

On May 23, 1985, however, Mr. Wilson announced in his budget speech: **"We will move immediately to close the plants."** Notwithstanding Mr. Mulroney's promises, there were no new industries in the area, let alone high tech industries, but nevertheless the plants were closed and abandoned. Within days of Mr. Wilson's announcement, workers began dismantling them.

No one should be surprised that the people of Nova Scotia felt betrayed. The *Ottawa Citizen* of June 8, 1985, reported how Bernie MacDonald, a mechanic in the Glace Bay plant, said of then Energy Minister Pat Carney:

> **"She came here and promised the plant would not be shut down until there were other jobs for us and we met with her yesterday and now all these promised jobs have been whittled down and gone to nothing."**

Clarence Routledge, a Glace Bay councillor, said he could not understand how the government could **"kick us when we're down."**

By then, the people of Atlantic Canada began to appreciate what Mr. Mulroney really meant when he promised to burden them with prosperity.

The manner in which the Mulroney Conservatives dealt with Atlantic Canada deserves chapters of examination. There are few better examples of "contrary performance." However, Michael Wilson's 1986 Budget, demands immediate attention.

When Mr. Wilson rose in the House of Commons on February 26, 1986 to present his second budget, he began thus:

"I want to speak frankly to this House, and to the people of Canada.

My message today is a serious one, and in many ways not pleasant. But it must be said. And it must be understood.

We have made tremendous progress together in the past 18 months. ...

But the mounting burden of public debt continues to threaten our future. It is growing faster than our ability to pay. It must be controlled."

Mr. Wilson then went on to prescribe some strong medicine. It certainly would not taste very good going down, but in return, he promised a speedy recovery for the patient.

First, the medicine.

The Mulroney team's promise to increase foreign aid spending to 0.6 per cent of GDP by 1990 was shelved. The new promise was to reach that percentage by the mid 1990's. That promise, too, was shelved in due course.

The Mulroney team's promise to increase significantly defence spending was the next promise to go out the window. Real annual increases in defence spending would be curtailed to below 1984 levels. Total public service employment was to be cut by 15,000 by the 1990-91 fiscal year. Programs such as the Canadian Home Insulation program and the Katimavik program were terminated.

Spending on Economic and Regional Development was to be cut by 11.1%. This followed a 15.4% cut the previous year. Those cuts to Economic and Regional Development are found at p. 31 of Mr. Wilson's *Fiscal Plan*. That is how the promise to inflict prosperity on the regions was being kept.

Mr. Wilson, at page 28 of his *Fiscal Plan*, described how beginning in the 1986-87 fiscal year, the indexation factor for Established Program Financing was being reduced by 2 percentage points per year.

This fairly innocuous entry in the Fiscal Plan was, in reality, a time bomb, threatening the future of our most important social program. Established Program Financing, otherwise known as EPF, is the vehicle the federal government uses to help the provinces fund post-secondary education and health care. We saw how candidate Mulroney promised — no, not merely promised, but vowed — to increase federal funding for health care to 50 per cent of total costs, and beyond. Now, with Wilson's 1986 Budget, the exact opposite was being done.

Here are a few paragraphs from a report of the National Council of Welfare, a federal government agency, entitled *Funding Health and Higher Education: Danger Looming*, Spring 1991.

> **Originally, federal support for health and higher education was to keep pace each year with overall growth in the economy. Since 1986, however, the support has been cut back as a result of a series of unilateral decisions by the federal government aimed at reducing the deficit.**
>
> **One of the unavoidable consequences of the cutbacks is that the cash portion of basic federal support has begun to decline. If the current trend continues, every last penny of federal cash for health and higher education under the 1977 fiscal arrangements will disappear within a few years.**
>
> **The consequences would be particularly severe for medicare. Instead of a national system of public health insurance that is more or less the same everywhere, we could wind up with 12 vastly different provincial and territorial medicare systems. Extra billing by doctors and hospital user fees —**

practices all but wiped out by the Canada Health Act of 1984 — would almost certainly reappear in some jurisdictions.

When and how did this problem first arise? The answer appears on page 17 of the report:

The first change in the overall EPF formula came in the 1986 budget as part of the federal government's efforts to reduce the size of the deficit. Ottawa announced unilaterally that EPF entitlements would no longer grow with the economy as a whole, but would be held to economic growth minus two percentage points.

This was the first step down the slippery slope. It was taken by Mr. Wilson in his 1986 budget, with the Prime Minister's full support, even though Mr. Mulroney knew that it broke the promise he made to the people of Nova Scotia and all Canadians about increasing the federal government's support for health care. This first cutback was followed by others in subsequent budgets.

In his 1989 budget, Mr. Wilson announced another one per cent decrease in the growth of EPF transfers, effective January 1, 1990. Increases would now be held to economic growth minus three percentage points. In his 1990 budget, Mr. Wilson announced a complete freeze on per capita EPF transfers for two years. In his 1991 budget, Mr. Wilson announced that the freeze was being extended for another three years. These changes removed billions of dollars in funding to the provinces for health and post-secondary education.

In the March 1993 issue of the C.D. Howe Institute magazine *Commentary*, there appeared an article entitled "Stealing the Emperor's Clothes: Deficit Offloading and National Standards in Health Care." The authors, Paul Booth and Barbara Johnston wanted to find out how much the federal government has offloaded, or cut back on health care funding. They calculated that for the 1991-92 fiscal year alone, federal government cuts of $1.7 billion **"can be attributed specifically to health care."** They found that **"the federal contribution to provincial social programs is declining as a share of the total cost of these programs."**

We saw how candidate Mulroney promised to increase the federal government's share of the health care program. At page 6 of the article we learn that the federal government's share of total health care spending **"declined from about 21 percent in fiscal year 1987/88 to about 15 percent in 1991/92."**

Has the federal government been cutting back on health care expenditures only in the same proportion that it is cutting other expenditures? According to Boothe and Johnston, the answer is No.

Over the four-year period 1989-1992, other federal programs grew by 25.5 percent while transfers for health grew by only 0.6 percent. Clearly, federal transfers for health have borne a disproportionate share of the burden of federal deficit reduction.

...despite the rhetoric from Ottawa, the health care system has been targeted as one of the main areas to bear the burden of federal deficit reduction.

Health care, the most sacred of sacred trusts for Brian Mulroney, has been hammered the hardest by his team according to this article.

The Mulroney Conservatives, of course, argue that they transfer tax points as well as cash to the provinces. Boothe and Johnston mince no words in showing the specious nature of this argument.

The tax points in question are included in the calculation of provincial tax payable on personal income tax returns. They are not included by the federal government in its own expenditure or revenue calculations. Nor have past transfers of tax points between federal and provincial governments been treated as anything other than provincial revenue. The federal government's rhetoric claiming that it is "giving" the provinces this tax revenue anew each year strains credulity — particularly since the actual collection is left to the provinces themselves.

These observations are not from some lunatic fringe group. They are contained in a publication put out by the acclaimed C.D. Howe Institute.

What have been the effects of these cutbacks? A national health care system under severe strain! And it all started in 1986, when the members of Mr. Mulroney's team decided to offload their deficit problem onto the provinces by cutting back on health care funding.

What about all the campaign promises Mr. Mulroney made about the sanctity of our health care system? We saw in the *Ottawa Citizen* of August 24, 1983, that Mulroney promised to split medicare costs with the provinces on a 50-50 basis if elected to office. Those promises were killed and buried.

What does Mr. Mulroney now allege happened between 1984 and 1993? **"We kept our word"**, he declares. On Sunday, June 13, 1993, Kim Campbell, in her acceptance speech to the Conservative leadership convention, thanked Brian Mulroney for showing the Conservative Party **"how to win."**

Finding herself bolted to her mentor's policies and record, how will Ms. Campbell now deal with the problems facing our health care system? Let's look at the *Globe and Mail* of April 30, 1993.

> **Conservative leadership candidate Kim Campbell says she is ready to preside over a new era in medicare, in which Canadians could be required to pay for medical services they use.**
>
> **That fundamental change to the health care system is just one measure of where Ms. Campbell believes a future prime minister could be forced to take the country.**
>
> **Asked whether she would consider user fees for medicare — a challenge to the whole system of universality in Canadian social services — Ms. Campbell said she would. "If it was the consensus of working with the provinces on how to rejig our social programs, then yes."**

Later she said that though she does not believe user fees will help control medicare costs, she thinks that perhaps one province could be allowed to impose them as an experiment. **"Perhaps it might make sense to let one province experiment with them to demonstrate the fact they don't work."** (*Gazette*, May 4/93) Which Canadian citizens will be the lucky guinea pigs Ms.

Campbell will experiment on in order to show that user fees don't work? Will they be citizens of her own province, British Columbia.

Ms. Campbell was an inner member of the Mulroney team which withheld billions of dollars from the provinces that should have been going to health care. She supported the decision of Mr. Mulroney and Mr. Wilson to reduce the federal government's share of health care costs, notwithstanding earlier promises. Now she promises to do even better by not only continuing the policy of offloading, but by moving to undermine the very foundations of our healthcare system.

There was, of course, more to the Mulroney team's 1986 budget than expenditure reductions and downloading. There were also more tax increases from the Finance Minister-Michael "we would not raise taxes" Wilson.

First, there was another increase to the federal sales tax. Effective April 1, 1986, it would increase from 11% to 12%, the third such increase in 18 months. The "temporary" high income surtax was staying and would be joined by a new 3 per cent surtax for everyone. There were, of course, tax increases for tobacco and alcohol, along with a surtax for corporations. But corporations got something that individuals didn't get when saddled with their surtax. Their basic tax rate was to be reduced from 36 per cent to 33 per cent by 1989.

That was the medicine Mr. Wilson prescribed to deal with the deficit. Would the patient get better as a result? It would, Wilson assured Canadians. By the 1990-91 fiscal year, the deficit would be slashed to $22 billion. Is that what happened? Mr. Wilson was not even close. In 1990-91, the deficit was $30.5 billion.

In his 1986 Budget, Mr. Wilson said also that the government's financial requirements — what it actually had to borrow — would be $11 billion for the 1990-91 fiscal year. When that year came, they were actually $23.8 billion. That was the result of Wilson's so-called "realistic" medium term plan. The government had to borrow over twice as much as Wilson had predicted. We have seen why Kim Campbell said: **"I am totally supportive of the Government's economic direction first laid out by Michael Wilson and consistently followed since then."** (April 29, 1993, *Press Release*) The only consistent aspect of Mr. Wilson's policies is that they, like his deficit projections, were consistent failures.

Let's turn briefly to Mr. Wilson's budget of February 18, 1987 — his third. The tone in 1987 was much moderated. The deficit battle, he said, was proceeding splendidly, requiring only a few adjustments. Those adjustments were more tax increases. The air transportation tax was increased. The excise tax on gasoline was increased. The excise tax on cigarettes was increased. The federal sales tax was expanded once again. While expanding the scope of the sales tax, Wilson complained, at page 13 of his speech, that it needed reform because **"it is a silent killer of jobs."**

It was in this budget that Mr. Wilson reached anything that could remotely be called success. He projected a deficit of $29.3 billion for the 1987-88 fiscal year and actually brought it in at $28.1 billion. Unfortunately, it would climb in every subsequent year, reaching $35.5 billion in the 1992-93 fiscal year. The reason for this reversal was the general election of 1988.

The deficit, which had been no big problem during the 1984 campaign, a priority in 1985, and a crisis in 1986, was put on the back burner in 1987, and declared tamed for election year 1988. But Wilson's 1988 budget, which properly belongs in our examination of the 1988 general election campaign, will have to take a temporary back seat as we turn our attention to some of the other dubious achievements of the Mulroney Conservatives' first term in office.

8.

CONSTITUTIONAL REVISIONISM

NATIONAL RECONCILIATION WAS ADVANCED as one of the key objectives of the new Mulroney team in the Throne Speech on November 5, 1984. Let us look at how the Mulroneyites went about achieving national reconciliation.

On May 28, 1993, in a speech before the Confederation Club in Ottawa, Prime Minister Brian Mulroney gave his version of what transpired since 1980 on the constitutional front. He began with a warning which forecast his strategy:

"Revisionism and myth-making are constant companions of political controversy."

Virtually everything he uttered subsequently proves the truth of that statement. Though he said, **"Today, I want to speak from the record"**, his imagination immediately took over and he forgot the record.

Let us start with his own attitude to the agreement reached by nine provinces and the federal government to patriate the Constitution with an amending formula and a Charter of Rights. That agreement was reached on November 5, 1981, and the Constitution was patriated the following year.

We have seen how Mr. Mulroney had *supported* Prime Minister Trudeau's earlier attempt to patriate the Constitution unilaterally. In his May 28, 1993 Ottawa speech, Mr. Mulroney admits that he was generally supportive of Mr. Trudeau's initiative in 1980, but that when it came to the patriation package agreed to on November 5, 1981, his opposition was firm and resolute.

"The myth created by some revisionists, however — that my generally-supportive position expressed in 1980 implied assent to all aspects of the final product — which had been modified often during the process and into which the now infamous notwithstanding clause had been inserted at the last moment, sometime between November 4 and November 5, 1981 — is false. In fact, I had specifically rejected any

THE SHOW MUST NOT GO ON

approach that reduced the powers of the Quebec National Assembly, which this final amendment did."

It is not the alleged myth which is false, but rather Mulroney's statement. The truth is that Mr. Mulroney *supported* the agreement of November 5, 1981. He thought it was legitimate and that it represented a national consensus.

In his book *Where I Stand*, Mr. Mulroney reprinted a series of speeches he gave while a private citizen. One of those speeches was made to the fund-raising dinner for the Regional Federation of Servcom Associations of the North Shore, at Hôtel Le Manoir, Baie Comeau, Quebec, on November 14, 1981. That is nine days *after* the patriation agreement of November 5, 1981.

The speech is reprinted on pages 62-66 of his book. At page 65, Mr. Mulroney says:

"But if Mr. Trudeau feels victorious, he should remember the words of Churchill, who, God knows, knew defeat and disappointment and finally the most exalting moments: 'In victory, magnanimity.'"

That is what the book says. But that is *not* what Mr. Mulroney himself said on November 14, 1981 in Baie Comeau. *The Halifax Chronicle-Herald* of November 24, 1981, printed large extracts of his November 14th speech. It reports Mr. Mulroney as follows:

"But, if Mr. Trudeau today feels victorious - <u>and why not? - did he not ably negotiate a national consensus which is really 'legitimate'?</u> he should remember the words of Churchill, who, God knows, knew defeat and disappointment and finally the most exalting moments: 'In victory, magnanimity.'"

When he reprinted the speech in his book, Mr. Mulroney deleted the words: " - and why not? - did he not ably negotiate a national consensus which is really 'legitimate'?" They vanish, as if never spoken. There is no subtlety to his revisionism — don't refine history, abolish it.

CONSTITUTIONAL REVISIONISM

Nine days after Trudeau and nine provincial premiers agreed on the patriation of the Constitution - an agreement to which Premier Rene Levesque refused assent, Mr. Mulroney said of Prime Minister Trudeau:

"did he not ably negotiate a national consensus which is really 'legitimate'"

That is what he said! In Mr. Mulroney's own words, the November 5, 1981 patriation agreement was **"legitimate,"** it was **"ably negotiated,"** and it represented **"a national consensus."** That stand, which he took in November, 1981, disappears from his 1983 book, *Where I Stand*. And now, in 1993, he says the suggestion that he supported the agreement is **"a myth"** and **"false."** He now says that the agreement was actually an **"ominous moment in the evolution of the Canadian Federation."**

Was Mr. Mulroney speaking his mind on November 14, 1981, when he said the agreement was legitimate and represented a national consensus? Or is he telling the truth today, when he says he had always opposed the agreement because it lacked legitimacy? Which is it?

This alteration of what he stated on November 14, 1981, was Mr. Mulroney's first foray into constitutional revisionism and myth-making. He started in 1983 and has kept it up ever since. In his speech of May 1993, instead of admitting that he had supported the patriation agreement, Mr. Mulroney declared that any such assertions are false, and then approvingly quotes Ernest Manning, who called the agreement **"a ticking constitutional time bomb."**

As we continue with our examination of the record, let's keep in mind how Mr. Mulroney was trying to falsify it even before presenting himself to the electorate for the first time. What is inexplicable is the way Mr. Mulroney doggedly and relentlessly defends a story he knows is not true. Apart from this *Chronicle-Herald* article, we had not seen a statement by Mr. Mulroney himself that he supported the patriation agreement of November, 1981. His support, however, was no secret to those who knew him.

THE SHOW MUST NOT GO ON

In a January 25, 1990, *Ottawa Citizen* article, Peter Blaikie, former national president of the Progressive Conservative Party, is quoted as saying:

> "I don't think it's any secret that during the period '80 through '83, Brian Mulroney was very supportive of Pierre Trudeau, ...He was one of the cheerleaders for all that ... and the revisionism now is absolutely staggering."

Following Mulroney's Ottawa speech of May 28, 1993, Mr. Blaikie said:

> "If one wants to search for revisionism, there is no greater revisionism than Brian Mulroney's own (on that period) when he was absolutely a fervent supporter of Pierre Trudeau's position. Basically, so was I." (*Montreal Gazette*, June 1/93)

Jeffrey Simpson, in the *Globe and Mail* of January 4, 1990, wrote:

> "[Mulroney's] outrageous distortion is too great to let go unchallenged. I remember as if it were yesterday a long lunch at the Mount Royal Club in Montreal January 1981, with private citizen Brian Mulroney, in which he went on at great length against the "community of communities" approach to Canada of then-Conservative leader Joe Clark. In the course of that animated soliloquy, Mr. Mulroney said emphatically that Prime Minister Pierre Trudeau, faced with a separatist government in Quebec, would have no choice but to bring home the Constitution over Quebec's objections.
>
> Later on, when the patriation debate heated up, Mr. Mulroney again said privately that he supported what the Liberals were doing, given the circumstances that presented themselves at the time in Quebec. For Mr. Mulroney to say now that the whole exercise was done by people celebrating "in striped pants" is a gross perversion of his own attitudes."

Perhaps Mr. Mulroney believes he can continue the deception, notwithstanding these observations by others, because he thinks he

CONSTITUTIONAL REVISIONISM

is nowhere on the record. He is, however, on the record, in the *Halifax Chronicle-Herald* of November 24, 1981. He is on the record as saying of Mr. Trudeau: **"did he not ably negotiate a national consensus which is really 'legitimate'."** Those are his words. Twelve years later speaking for the record, he denies the record.

In retrospect, it is not surprising that the constitutional talks, when led by a man so shifty on constitutional principles, were doomed to failure. They started, however, cautiously and innocently enough.

In December, 1985, Bourassa's Liberal government replaced Levesque's separatist administration. As discussions began between Ottawa and the provinces, there was no hint of urgency. Gil Rémillard, Quebec Minister of Intergovernmental Affairs, said that without some indication of a solution, he wasn't particularly interested in engaging in constitutional talks. He said: **"Without that, we'd stay where we are."** (*Globe and Mail*, Aug. 5/86) This observation brought no gasps of dismay, no anguished cries of betrayal, from anyone, anywhere.

The federal government's pointman on this portfolio, Senator Lowell Murray, was very candid about the mood of the country in early 1987:

"I don't think there is any interest whatsoever from the population of the country on the Constitution — none whatsoever ...It's just not an issue."(*Toronto Star*, Mar. 4/87)

Senator Murray was right — there was no interest whatsoever, not even in Quebec. Although interest was low, the Constitution nevertheless remained a potentially explosive issue if demogogically stirred up. This was clearly recognized by Senator Murray, when he said:

"...we do not want to embark on any formal negotiations unless we are convinced that the chances for success are good. We must spare the country unnecessary agony." (*Maclean's*, Aug. 25/86)

In retrospect, "unnecessary agony" turned out to be the exactly right way to describe what in fact happened over the next 6 years.

Early in 1987, Senator Murray's view had not changed.

THE SHOW MUST NOT GO ON

> "We're not going to go into formal negotiations unless we think there's a very good chance of succeeding," Murray said. "We don't want another failure. We think it'd be very bad for the country." (*Toronto Star*, Mar. 4/87)

He certainly had it right at that time. Opening this portfolio and failing, for whatever reason, would be very bad for the country.

The risks were very high, but soon they were taken. Who chose to assume those risks? Well, part of the answer can be found in an interview Senator Murray gave to Don Braid, which appeared in the *Montreal Gazette*, on Sept. 9, 1986. Apparently, it was up to Senator Murray to advise the Prime Minister whether a deal was possible before the next election, or whether it should be put off until much later.

The prime minister **"would also want to hear from me, from a person in whose political judgment he has some confidence, if it's not on. I hope I don't have to tell him that, but I'll do so if that's my judgment."**

We can only deduce that Senator Murray, in whose political judgment the PM had confidence, and who is now an advisor and confidant of Ms. Campbell, at some point advised that formal negotiations were warranted. Or did Mr. Mulroney reject Murray's judgment? In either case, the negotiations proceeded.

Quebec's goals were well-known. Its five demands had long been in the public domain. The federal government, on the other hand, was tight-lipped about its position. What appeared in the public domain from Ottawa was a commitment to broker a deal, but there was no information on what the federal government was or was not willing to contribute. Only when the Meech Lake Accord was struck on April 30, 1987, were Canadians made aware that the bottom line for the Mulroney team was Quebec's five conditions plus. Even Bourassa was shocked at what had transpired at Meech Lake.

> "We didn't expect, after 20 years, to reach an agreement. Then suddenly, without warning, there it is: an agreement." (*Toronto Star*, May 4/87)

Bourassa confirmed that as far as he was concerned, there was no urgency.

> "We could have waited until next year, we could have waited until after the next federal election,...
>
> "We were under no pressure; I was serene. But when I saw that it was falling to us piece by piece, I said to myself: Bien voila, there it is." (*Toronto Star*, May 4/87)

Years later, Ghislain Fortin, former Senior Advisor to both Bourassa and Claude Ryan, and one of those who helped draft Quebec's five conditions, admitted that he was astonished when Meech Lake was concluded.

> "I fell out of my chair when I learned (of the Meech Lake Accord) on April 30, 1987...I was of the view that it was too much for English Canada, ...I always felt it was something to (get) past the (1985) election.
>
> "If people had said no to Meech in 1987, we would have moved on to other things....Since it was accepted, it was blown beyond proportion... it became a symbol of what English Canada accepts." (*Globe and Mail*, March 9/90)

The Mulroneyites had, however, refused to move onto other things. They relentlessly pushed forward with Meech Lake and started a disastrous chain of events which culminated in a national referendum on October 26, 1992.

One of the elements of the Meech Accord which caused the greatest acrimony was the recognition of Quebec, *within the body* of the Constitution, as a distinct society. This had not been one of Quebec's five demands. Quebec had been seeking recognition as a distinct society *within the preamble* of the Constitution. For those with short memories, refer back to the following newspaper articles:
- Southam News byline, *Ottawa Citizen*, July 12, 1986
- Joel Ruimy, *Toronto Star*, March 4, 1987
- Eugene Forsey, *Globe and Mail*, March 17, 1987

- Jeffrey Simpson, *Globe and Mail,* April 19, 1987

All these articles described how Quebec wanted recognition in the preamble. Lest Quebec's demands escape the attention of the federal government negotiators, *La Presse,* on April 25, 1987, only days before the Meech-fest was due to begin, printed a large chart of Premier Bourassa's demands. One of those demands, according to *La Presse,* was

> **Reconnaissance, en préambule de la constitution, du fait que le Québec est une SOCIETE DISTINCTE.**

This would have been acceptable to Mr. Mulroney's predecessor government and to most of Meech's most vocal critics, including Clyde Wells, Frank McKenna and Sharon Carstairs. But entering the meeting with the demand of recognition within a preamble, and leaving it with that recognition within the text of the Constitution itself, Bourassa had every reason to be pleased.

What of the federal negotiators? Was this raising of the stakes a make or break item for Bourassa? In retrospect, it is clear that had Meech met Quebec's five demands as originally and publicly presented, the course of the debate would have been very different. If it had been a bottom line item, most would agree with Ghislain Fortin that it would have been preferable had Meech failed on April 30, 1987, to what has occurred to date. If it had remained in the preamble, Meech may have passed.

The willingness of the Mulroney team to embrace so quickly this new demand of Bourassa's, was one of two crucial and fatal errors in political judgement. The second error, of course, was the outright dismissal of any public participation.

When Senator Murray, the Mulroney team's chief negotiator, reported to the Senate on May 5, 1987, he was proud of what had been achieved.

> **"...the accord is an eloquent demonstration of the government's commitment to make national reconciliation a basic principle of our political and constitutional existence." (*Senate Debates,* p. 932)**

He then explained what would come next: a first ministers' conference to ratify the legal text, followed by resolutions in Parliament

CONSTITUTIONAL REVISIONISM

and all legislative assemblies. Conspicuously absent was any role for the people of Canada. Although the terms **"egregious error"** and **"seamless web"** had yet to be coined by Senator Murray, the die had been cast.

On June 2, 1987, the eleven participants met at the Langevin Block to ratify the legal text. Nineteen hours later, at dawn the following day, they staggered out, dazed, but "successful." Canadians were amazed by this negotiating technique, but little did they know that it was but a prelude to a whole new and astonishing style that was to turn negotiating into some kind of casino or carnival game.

On the evening of June 4, Prime Minister Mulroney addressed the nation on the Constitution.

> **"I speak to you tonight at a time of renewed purpose for our country, at a moment of renewed unity for our people. Tonight, Canada is whole again, the Canadian family is together again, and the nation is one again."**

Mulroney's declaration that **"Canada is whole again"**, simply by agreement of eleven people, will join other world-class errors of political judgment.

In a speech he gave on November 14, 1980, Mr. Mulroney stated definite ideas about how governments should go about amending constitutions.

> **"The debate would be entirely open to the public at all times. *There would be no sessions behind closed doors.* Canadians could see and judge those who have been elected to serve them and determine if, in the interest of a more generous country, they have really answered an urgent and irresistible call to grandeur."** (*Where I Stand*, pp. 61-2)

"There would be no sessions behind closed doors" was so crucial to Brian Mulroney, that he italicized the passage in *Where I Stand*, the only such italicisation in the entire book. Yet when the deed was done, it was done entirely behind closed doors. There had been no open sessions — not a single one.

With the agreement now in the open, the citizens of some provinces were asked to participate in public hearings by their governments prior to ratification, but others were not. The Quebec and Saskatchewan legislatures quickly approved the deal, holding no hearings. In Ottawa, the Joint Senate-House of Commons hearings quickly dissolved into a charade after Senator Murray told the members what the Mulroney team expected of them:

> "...the Accord is a seamless web and an integrated whole...it should not be lightly tampered with....Your public hearings will ensure that the text of the amendment is carefully scrutinized before adoption. If it should come to light that there are egregious errors in the drafting, we would have an opportunity to address them, while bearing in mind that any change would have to meet the test of unanimity." (Issue #2, pp. 10 & 17.

Reporters, turning to their dictionaries, found that **"egregious"**, coming immediately after **"egomania"** and **"egotism"**, meant **"shocking, remarkable...standing out from the flock."** Andre Ouellet expressed the frustration of all Liberal members when he said:

> "...the government's position is that the hearings should be held to publicize the accord and not to change it. Our position is the reverse — that the hearings should lead to some changes." (*Toronto Star*, Aug. 9/87)

Unfortunately for the Accord and for the country, this was not to be. Mulroney and Murray were the engineers on this constitutional train. They had no intention of taking their hands off the throttle and the train was going non-stop.

No one was surprised when Senator Murray concluded, in September 1987, that the Joint Committee had discovered no egregious errors. He warned that if the Accord were reopened to accommodate even one change, this **"would lead to irresistible pressure for others, and the accord would soon unravel."** The consequences to future generations would be **"grave"** he declared. (*Ottawa Citizen*, Sept. 10, 1987)

In the following years, any opposition to the Accord was either ridiculed or wished away. Amendments introduced in the Senate by

CONSTITUTIONAL REVISIONISM

the Liberal Party were denounced as **"killer amendments"** by Senator Murray, when in fact, they could have saved the Accord. Changes of governments in New Brunswick, Manitoba and Newfoundland caused the Mulroney team no concern. The Accord was going to pass: that was all there was to it! That public support had dropped from 56% to 28% (Gallup, *Montreal Gazette,* April 29, 1988) was not relevant because this was a deal between 11 men. As long as it stayed in those few select hands, there was no danger of any change.

When the *Ottawa Citizen* called for the Accord to be reopened, Senator Murray answered that to reopen it

> **"...for amendment would lead to its unravelling and destruction. I could not think of a better way of insulting Quebecers and indeed, all Canadians, than by scuttling an agreement that achieves Quebec's willing acceptance of our constitution and ends Quebec's isolation from the constitutional process."** (*Citizen,* **June, 1988**)

This new weapon in the arsenals of threats deployed by the creators of Meech - the Accord's failure would insult Quebecers - is a perfect example of a self-fulfilling prophecy.

The Prime Minister called upon the rest of Canada **"to say yes to Quebec"** (*Toronto Star,* June 15, 1988), implying that a rejection of Meech did not mean just saying No to the deal, it meant saying No to Quebec. When Bernard Valcourt appeared before the New Brunswick hearings, he advised: **"you must resist the opportunity to use the Accord to say no to Quebec."** (*Globe and Mail,* Feb. 15, 1989.)

When Bourassa used the notwithstanding clause and Filman responded by withdrawing Manitoba's support, Senator Murray concluded that Filman had acted **"in the heat of the moment"** and urged the Premier to send the Accord to committee for the required hearings. (*Toronto Star,* Dec. 20, 1988) Soon thereafter, Mr. Mulroney confidently declared that Meech was **"a done deal"** (*Montreal Gazette,* Feb. 27, 1989), but he provided no information on how he would deal with hesitant premiers.

Though he spoke confidently about the future of Meech, Mr. Mulroney stepped up his attacks on its opponents, both real and imagined. On April 6, 1989, during the Throne Speech debate, he launched a blistering attack on the 1982 Constitution and, by association, its creators. He lamented that because it had not been approved by the Quebec National Assembly, it did not bring unity. And since it contained the notwithstanding clause, it did not protect individual rights.

"A constitution that does not bring Canadians together, that is not accepted by all Canadians, and a constitution that does not protect the inalienable and imprescriptible individual rights of individual Canadians is not worth the paper it is written on." (*Hansard*, p. 153)

Never mind that in 1981, he said it was **"able negotiated"**, represented a **"national consensus"** and was **"legitimate"**. Eight years later, it was not worth the paper it was written on. Like a vaudeville magician, he was tearing it up so as to be able to claim credit for putting it together again.

But he failed. The dice were rolled, the Meech Lake Agreement failed and the Mulroneyites went into shock. Reeling, they tried again with the Charlottetown Accord, but that was shot down by voters in every region of the country. Why was it so overwhelmingly rejected? What was the referendum all about?

Ms. Kim Campbell knew what the referendum was about. Speaking at Harvard University on November 10, 1992, she declared:

"It was about the Canadian political process and what Canadians think about it, their ignorance about it, their lack of understanding of how the Canadian political system works." (Transcript)

Did she ever consider the possiblity that those Canadians who voted in the referendum on October 26, 1992, knew only too well how the Canadian political system had been working and that they were fed-up. It was not the ignorance of the Canadian people which placed the country at risk. The ignorance resided within the Mulroneyite camp - with Mulroney, Clark, Campbell and the rest - who thought they could scare the people of Canada into voting for the Charlottetown Accord.

Mulroney scowled; Clark threatened; Campbell stamped her foot. The spin doctors spun by day and by night. The big dollars came down like an avalanche. But the people weren't buying. They knew how to say, **"NO."**

9.

PATRONAGE FROM THE "PINOCCHIO OF POLITICS"

RICHARD CLEROUX IS A VETERAN Parliament hill reporter, who for many years covered Parliament Hill for the Globe and Mail. Late in 1992, speaking before "The Media Club", he said:

> "We here in Canada between 1984 and 1992 have lived through the most corruption-ridden federal government in our history. More members of Parliament have been charged and convicted of corruption, breach of trust and conspiracy than at any time in our 125 years as a nation." (*Hill Times*, Dec. 3/92)

Examination of each and every incident to which Mr. Cleroux refers is far, far beyond our scope, but let's look at some of the highlights, as well as other items of interest, during the Mulroneyites first term in office.

Let's start with Mulroney's first Minister of Defence, Robert Coates. After spending $139,000 to redecorate his office, but before getting an opportunity to enjoy fully his new grandeur Coates stepped down from Cabinet on February 12, 1985. The resignation of Canada's Minister of National Defence followed reports about where he turned for R&R while inspecting our troops in West Germany.

Next, we had the resignation of the Minister of Fisheries, John Fraser, on Monday, September 23, 1985. That resignation had its beginnings when the new minister decided that a million tins of tuna, which his own inspectors had found to be unfit for human consumption, and which had been rejected by the Department of Defence, and also by a humanitarian relief agency as unfit for the starving people of Ethiopia, should be allowed onto the shelves of Canadians supermarkets. That was a serious error in judgment. Mr. Fraser resigned. Mulroney's view of Mr. Fraser's real sin, however, was not his decision that rancid tuna was good enough for Canadians, but his remarks that Mulroney had not been telling the truth.

The story began on Tuesday, September 17, 1985, when CBC's *Fifth Estate* revealed how the Minister of Fisheries had dealt with the tainted tuna. During Question Period the following day, Mr. Mulroney defended his minister and claimed that the health and safety of Canadians had never been at risk, although people had been very sick from it all across the country. Suggestions that he dismiss Mr. Fraser from cabinet were rejected out of hand. The following day, Thursday, September 19, the minister ordered the rancid tuna off store shelves. The next day, the Prime Minister told a press conference that the first he had heard of the tainted tuna was when the television program originally had been aired. Unfortunately for him, on that same Friday his fisheries minister said: **"The issue was in the Prime Minister's Office in detailed form a couple of weeks ago."** (*Ottawa Citizen*, Sept. 24/85)

Only one outcome was possible. On Monday, September 23, Mr. Fraser tendered his resignation, which Mulroney accepted. As Liberal MP Brian Tobin said the following day, it was interesting **"that the Prime Minister defended the Minister of Fisheries and Oceans when the Minister's actions threatened the public good. However, he swiftly canned that same Minister when the Minister's actions threatened the Prime Minister personally."** (*Hansard*, Sept. 24/85, p. 6916)

That should have been the end of it, but it was not. On Wednesday morning, September 25, Conservative MP Fred McCain, in whose riding the Star-Kist plant was located, told Robert Fife of Canadian Press that he had long been raising the problems the plant was having with federal fisheries inspectors, who were labelling tuna as rancid. He said: **"I did bring it up, I'm sure in caucus during discussions since September of last year...."**

A short while later he phoned the reporter back and said he had been mistaken and that he had never raised the issue at caucus or with the Prime Minister's Office. When asked by the puzzled reporter: **"Did the Prime Minister's Office talk to you about it?"**, McCain answered: **"Yes, they did. I have doubled checked it, but, no, I did not raise it...."**

PATRONAGE FROM THE "PINOCCHIO OF POLITICS"

After that conversation, Mr. McCain phoned the reporter back yet again, and said:

"I say unequivocally the following:

There was no pressure by the prime minister's office on me to make any change in any statement which I have ever made now or at any time in the past."

A partial transcript of the three telephone calls appeared in the *Ottawa Citizen* of September 26, 1985.

When questioned in the House of Commons about this latest episode in Tunagate, Mr. Mulroney denied everything, and charged **"the Liberal Party... has no respect for the truth or for Parliament."**

Six months later, during an interview with *The New York Times*, Mr. Mulroney gave his considered and "truthful" perspective of Tunagate.

"...when the matter was brought to my attention, bang, immediately the minister's resignation was secured."

We now know that this statement was absolutely false. No one was shocked to hear Liberal MP John Nunziata's charge: **"The Prime Minister is a compulsive liar."** (*Ottawa Citizen*, Mar. 22/86) It is important to recall that Mr. Nunziata's statement was made outside the Chamber, beyond the immunity that exists within the House of Commons. But no one seriously thought that the Prime Minister would launch an action for defamation or slander. They were right. Not only was there no slander suit, there was not even a request for a retraction by any of the Mulroneyites.

But let's get back to the final week in September of 1985. The week went from bad to worse when Mr. Marcel Masse, Minister of Communications, announced that he too was resigning from Cabinet because he was the subject of an inquiry concerning an alleged violation of the *Elections Act*. Fortunately for the Mulroney team, the allegations proved completely unfounded and Mr. Masse quickly rejoined his cabinet colleagues, though two of his campaign workers were convicted and fined. Unfortunately for the Mulroneyites, the initial resignation of Mr. Masse led to another episode where Mulroney's veracity was once again placed in doubt.

In the House of Commons, on September 26, 1985, Mr. Mulroney stated that he had no prior knowledge of his minister's problems, and neither had his staff. Responding to a question put by Liberal Leader, John Turner, Mulroney replied:

> "...I wish to assure him of two things. I had no prior knowledge of any kind; nor am I aware of anyone on my senior staff who might have had such knowledge." (*Hansard*, p. 7050)

That same day, Mr. Jerry Lampert, national director of the Conservative Party, told the media otherwise.

> **Lampert had said that although he did not inform Mulroney, "I had discussions, you know, with people in the prime minister's office...".**
>
> **Asked if they were senior aides, he replied: "Oh yes, senior PMO people."** (*Toronto Sun*, **Sept. 27/85**)

After the inconsistencies in the two versions of events had been headlined in the media, Mr. Lampert issued a letter of apology, saying he had been mistaken. Six months later, he resigned as national director of the Conservative Party.

These episodes, though always followed by a retraction or apology, spawned headlines such as **"The Pinocchio of Politics,"** a label that has followed Mr. Mulroney ever since.

That was not the end of the bad news in 1985 for the Mulroneyites. We had bank collapses, the first in more than 60 years. First it was the Canadian Commercial Bank on Labour Day, and then the Northland Bank, on September 30. Taxpayers were stuck with the bill while all the Mulroney ministers steadfastly denied any responsibility whatsoever. These banks could have collapsed on another planet as far as their responsibilities were concerned.

We had stories of the globe-trotting Minister of the Environment, Suzanne Blais-Grenier, who toured through northern France for 4 days in a chauffeur-driven government financed limousine, accompanied by her husband, her chief of staff and his girlfriend. Accord-

PATRONAGE FROM THE "PINOCCHIO OF POLITICS"

ing to the *Globe and Mail* of August 6, 1985, an External Affairs telegram described her husband **"as a civil servant and the companion of her chief of staff was called a consultant."**

When questions were raised in the House of Commons on October 4, 1985, about her expenses, Erik Neilsen, the Deputy Prime Minister, questioned the motives of those who perceived any wrongdoing:

> "I asked myself whether the motivation was not to arouse some kind of racism here, something... which I think is most regrettable." (*Hansard*, p. 7333)

More major league action involved corporate tax schemes. First there was the takeover of Gulf Canada by Olympia and York. When questioned on October 1, 1985, the Minister of Finance did not deny that Gulf Canada saved $1 billion in taxes through a favourable tax ruling. He refused to discuss the matter, saying: **"tax rulings are privileged matters between the Minister of National Revenue and the particular company concerned"**. (*Hansard*, p. 7203)

Then there was the takeover of Canada Trustco Mortgage Company by Genstar Financial Corporation. Genstar, needing money, floated a share issue. According to the *Ottawa Citizen* of December 2, 1985:

> **By the time the tax brains in the private sector had fiddled with this offering, it allowed a foreign bank a chance at windfall profits for a middleman role and offered some investors with $100,000 to invest an after-tax return on investment of more than 30 per cent a year, compounded, for five years.**
>
> **One leading tax specialist interviewed by The Citizen said the scheme was clearly legal but "scandalous"... Because of Genstar's unusual application of tax law the federal treasury will lose, at a maximum, about $10 million a year for five years, federal finance department officials said this week.**

What happened was that Genstar asked for, and received in advance, a binding tax ruling from Revenue Canada, allowing it to interpret creatively provisions in the *Income Tax Act* originally designed for family trusts. Revenue Canada is not obliged to provide binding advance rulings. Afterwards, legislation was introduced to close this loophole, but not before millions of tax had dollars poured out through it.

1985 was also the first full year in which Mr. Mulroney was able to show Canadians how he would do honour to them and the country by the splendid quality of his patronage appointments. The previous year hadn't brought much honour. A *Vancouver Sun* editorial of January 8, 1985, observed:

"Today people could be forgiven for wondering if Mr. Mulroney conned them on the patronage issue."

1985 wasn't much different from 1984. Here are some highlights. The *Toronto Sun* of April 23, 1985, described how the Department of Finance awarded a $234,000 untendered advertising contract to Lawson Murray Ltd. The Minister of Finance was Michael Wilson. The President of the company, Doug Lawson, was the brother-in-law of the Minister of Finance. The sister of the Minister of Finance was a director of the company. According to the *Toronto Sun*, Mr. Wilson said **"that came as news to him."** One of the two company vice presidents was Doug Robson, who was Wilson's riding association president and a former employee in Wilson's Ottawa office. All this was mere coincidence, nothing more!

The *Ottawa Citizen* of May 4, 1985, reported: **"The brother of External affairs Minister Joe Clark [Peter Clark] is the federal fundraising director for the Progressive Conservatives in Alberta and now receives all outside legal work awarded by the federal government's Calgary Olympic office."** This, too was mere coincidence.

In the pages of the *Ottawa Citizen* of May 8, 1985, the Joe Clark family saga continued. We learned that Peter Clark's wife had been named a temporary member of the National Parole Board. That appointment was later made permanent.

The *Ottawa Citizen* of June 4, 1985, reported how John Crosbie, Minister of Justice, presented the two-lawyer firm where his son, Chesley Crosbie, worked, with a contract to handle all government prosecutions under two federal fisheries acts and the Oil Pollution Prevention Regulations. Another son, Michael, worked for the law

PATRONAGE FROM THE "PINOCCHIO OF POLITICS"

firm of Chalker, Green and Rowe. His dad, the minister, made him legal agent in Newfoundland for *Income Tax Act* violations. Both sons were also made agents for the Canadian Mortgage and Housing Corporations. According to the *Toronto Sun* of June 4, the sons had been members of the bar only since 1983, and one of them had failed two years of law school. Nevertheless, they were made legal agents for the Government of Canada. The embarrassment for the government and Mr. Crosbie became so acute that both firms eventually resigned as federal legal agents. A few weeks after that withdrawal, however, both legal firms, according to the *Globe and Mail*, of August 20, 1985, were appointed as standing agents for the Federal Business Development Bank, at the direct request of the Justice Minister's office.

The *Globe and Mail* of June 7, 1985 told the story of John McMillan of Prince Edward Island. John McMillan had two brothers. One was Tourism Minister Thomas McMillan. The other was Charles McMillan, senior policy advisor to Prime Minister Mulroney. John McMillan was called to the Bar of P.E.I., went out to gain some work experience, and then two weeks later, was appointed legal agent in the province of Prince Edward Island for the government of Canada. According to the *Globe and Mail:*

Securing the appointment of legal agent was not all that difficult, Mr. McMillan recalls. He just picked up the telephone and called his brother Tom's office in Ottawa. Actually, he did not speak to Tom, he said, but to his executive assistant who just happened to be an old roommate from university days.

The *Globe and Mail* of September 4, 1985, reported that when Gayle Christie, a Conservative Party activist who was appointed to the board of directors of Air Canada, was asked about her credentials, she replied: **"Well, I can drive a car."** The same newspaper story revealed that the new directors appointed to the board of VIA Rail included two former PC candidates, the Quebec PC Party President, Mr. Mulroney's New Brunswick organizer during the leadership campaign, a member of the PC party's candidate selection committee, and two Toronto PC activists.

THE SHOW MUST NOT GO ON

The *Toronto Star* of September 12, 1985, reported how Mr. Sam Wakim, a university roommate of Mr. Mulroney, allegedly **"approached a number of Toronto law firms promising new government business if they hired him. Wakim eventually joined the Toronto law firm of Weir and Foulds, which later won $200,000 worth of government business previously handled by another firm."**

At year end, when Mr. Mulroney was asked whether it had been difficult to deal with all the controversies that surrounded his government during the years, particularly the scandals, he replied:

"Well, as it turns out it wasn't difficult because my integrity was questioned and it came out completely unsullied." (*Toronto Sun*, **Dec. 19/85**)

New Years Day, 1986, did not see the turning of a new page. The top headlines on New Year's Day announced the resignation from cabinet of Ms. Suzanne Blais-Grenier. Allegedly she was protesting her government's decision to let the Gulf refinery in Montreal close down, throwing 450 people out of work. Others, however, viewed it more as a pre-emptive strike by a minister who knew her days were numbered. The *Ottawa Citizen* of January 2, 1986, reviewing her accomplishments, reported:

When a truck spilled toxic PCB's on the Trans-Canada highway in April, Blais-Grenier told anxious reporters they would have to wait until she had put on some lipstick....

A month later, she faced the cameras and scribes again, this time to suggest the government might allow mining and lumbering in national parks.

The *Ottawa Citizen* of January 12, 1986, reported another departure. This time it was the firing of cabinet minister Roch LaSalle's special assistant, Frank Majeau. According to the article, Mr. Majeau had operated a nude dancer booking agency in 1983. One of his business partners was involved in the murder of a drug courier, **"who, court records show, once used Majeau's Toronto apartment as a drop-off point for cocaine."** That partner, Réal Simard, was convicted of mur-

PATRONAGE FROM THE "PINOCCHIO OF POLITICS"

der. Mr. Majeau himself had a criminal record, for assault with a weapon causing bodily harm. Though LaSalle and Majeau had been friends for nearly 25 years, Mr. LaSalle was apparently unaware of Majeau's background until alerted by the media.

As the Mulroneyites dipped in the polls, the team leader decided that the problem lay with the messenger, and not the team. The headline of the *Ottawa Citizen*, January 20, 1986, read: **"PM blames press for sagging popularity."** The article quotes Mr. Mulroney:

> **"We know what we're up against. We're not a bunch of children. We understand your (media's) obligations and we accept our own and we've got to get our message out and we're going to do it, you can be sure of that."**

How was the message to be sold? The partial answer is provided by a January 23, 1986, *Toronto Star* article headlined: **"PM's new strategy: Breakfast with Brian".** The new plan was to invite selected media leaders to join Mulroney at 24 Sussex for off-the-record breakfast chats. Mulroney's associate press secretary, Michel Gratton, said that the team leader

> **"... would like an opportunity to more directly explain his policies to the press. And he would also like to hear more directly from reporters as to why they have reacted negatively to some things."**

In the future, they were expected to react more constructively to things like Tunagate and Tory patronage.

Another part of the plan, according to the *Toronto Sun* of February 7, 1986, was,

> **to have some sort of "dial-a-date" arrangement between selected news reporters and certain cabinet ministers. By pairing ministers with friendly reporters they hope to get the good word out to the people of Canada.**

Also, a less subtle approach was employed. Press secretary Michel Gratton developed the annoying habit of asking female reporters who called requesting interviews with the PM for dates. Press aide, Bill Fox, left the following message for a columnist who wrote about Mulroney installing a jacuzzi at 24 Sussex: **"Tell him from me I'm going to rip** his (bleeping) lungs out." (*Ottawa Citizen*, Nov. 15/86) Were the threats, dial-a-dates, breakfast gabs and requests for dates with the media elites successful? Only the participants know the answer. What we do know, however, is that no one, no matter how hard they tried, could ignore the continuing and seemingly endless stories of cronyism, patronage and outright corruption.

In January 1986, it was revealed that Erik Neilsen, while an opposition MP in the 1960's, had eavesdropped on Liberal caucus meetings. In an interview he taped in 1973, he said: **"There was a method by which we knew every Wednesday what was said in the Liberal caucus word for bloody word."**

It was said that wires had been crossed when an electronic system was being installed, and the Tories took full advantage of this situation. They listened through headphones in a translation booth located in their own caucus. Though that is the official story, the *Globe and Mail* of February 4, 1986, reported that the House of Commons has no record of any crossed wires.

The *Ottawa Citizen* of February 5, 1986, carried a story about a House of Commons technician who alleged that **"communications devices in the Liberal caucus room had been 'deliberately tampered with'around the time of the Erik Neilsen eavesdropping affair."** The technician described how he found a microphone wire, **"that wasn't our work and wasn't our wire"** spliced into one of the junction boxes.

Was it innocently crossed wires, or deliberate wiretapping? Whichever, there was no innocence in its exploitation.

Remember how Mr. Neilsen railed when he discovered that Mr. Trudeau's office kept press clippings on Mr. Mulroney? That was one of the greatest violations of parliamentary ethics in history. Electronic eavesdropping on fellow parliamentarians, on the other hand, was ordinary course of business. When raised in the House of Commons, on January 30, 1986, Mr. Neilsen said there had been anonymous plain brown envelopes flying around the hill for decades, as if this was the same thing. The Prime Minister defended Mr. Neilsen to the limit, saying he had **"served his country honourably"** and found that **"There is no allegation of illegality, or even impropriety."** (*Hansard*, pp. 10327 and 10332)

PATRONAGE FROM THE "PINOCCHIO OF POLITICS"

This time the Mulroneyites were too tightly cornered for even them to brass it out. After stalling and stonewalling for almost a week, Mr. Neilsen finally managed a half-hearted apology. On February 3, 1986, he told the House of Commons: **"I apologize to those who believe that proprieties were violated 25 years ago by my conduct."**

On March 9, 1986, Canadians learned that when loyal Tories competed for government jobs, they were spotted a lead, so that they would have a better chance at success. The *Toronto Star* of that day reported:

> **Conservative party members have been ordered hired as census commissioners in Ontario and Quebec even though they failed miserably on tests given to prospective candidates....**
>
> **They were hired on instructions from Supply and Services Minister Stewart McInnes even though in some cases candidates scored in the 20s on the test, sources said. A passing grade is 60 per cent.**

The article describes one case where,

> **a census area manager said, he had two candidates who had failed. He was ordered to pick one, he said.**
>
> **He was also referred a candidate who had already been told a starting date by his Conservative MP.**
>
> **The person scored zero on the test, and only on appeal was the candidate rejected.**

Was the government concerned about the revelations? The *Toronto Star* reports:
An aide to McInnes called the allegations "a non-issue".

It was a little harder, however, to put a positive spin on the letter Conservative MP Marcel Tremblay sent to party workers in late February of 1986. According to the *Globe and Mail* of March 6, the letter,

> **said contracts should be given to people who contributed to the 1984 election campaign, who belong to the Brian Mul-**

roney Club (a Quebec Tory fund-raising group) or who took part in a fund raiser in Mr. Tremblay's riding in October.

The letter described how there were over $1 billion in untendered government contracts every year. Attached to the letter was a list of 66 government projects in Mr. Tremblay's riding which would be awarded without public tender.

Mr. Tremblay, of course, sent out a second letter claiming that the first was sent in error. The Deputy Prime Minister, Erik Neilsen, said it was just a mistake, case closed. It was, however, difficult to pretend that this was an abberation. In 1986, Pierre Blouin, **"an advance man for Mulroney in Quebec during the 1984 election campaign,"** (*Ottawa Citizen*, Feb. 9/87) pleaded guilty to influence-peddling. He had been asking for a 6 per cent commission on a $1 million government contract. When asked for his reaction, **"Mulroney said the story was groundless.... 'That has been denied'..."** (*Toronto Star*, Feb. 8/87) Mulroney may have denied it, but he couldn't change the fact that one of his advance men had been charged and convicted of political corruption.

On March 7, 1986, the day following the release of Mr. Tremblay's letter, there was another revelation. This time it was the disclosure of a letter, dated January 6, 1986, signed by the Minister of State for Youth, Andrée Champagne, addressed to her colleagues in the PC caucus.

First, it described **"the significant diminution in youth-related spending (close to $100M since the election)."** This did not cause any excitement, even though it showed that Mulroney's election promise to treat youth unemployment very seriously had been junked. By now, however, broken Mulroney promises had become so commonplace that they raised nothing but cynical yawns.

But the letter continued:

2.5 of 4.5 million young Canadians (15-24) will be casting a vote for the first time in 1988. Support to the recruitment efforts of the PC Youth Federations will be a pre-writ priority for the Government.

So the priority of the government of Canada was not to find jobs for young people, but to recruit them into Conservative Party. The letter was marked **"secret."**

What were Canadians to make of this? They were asked to believe that once again, it was nothing but an honest mistake. Initially, Ms. Champagne suggested the letter might be a forgery. But later, she recognized her own signature and explained that the idea to use taxpayers' money to recruit young people into the Conservative Party was a mistake. The Minister apologized, said it was a mistake, and the government encouraged the inquisitive to move along to something else. When the curious lingered about, asking more questions, Mr. Mulroney's right hand man, Erik Neilsen, said:

"The Opposition has latched on to one aspect of the letter for which the Minister has apologized. It should ruddy well be satisfied with that...." (*Hansard*, **Mar. 19/86, p. 11354**)

We were caught; we apologized; that settled the matter!

In April and May of 1986, when the Sinclair Stevens affair emerged Mr. Neilsen, stonewalling all opposition questions, truly earned his nickname, **"Velcro-lips."**

Mr. Stevens, as we recall, was the Minister of Regional Industrial Expansion. He owned controlling interest in a company called York Centre Corporation. The shares of his company were put in a "blind trust" following the 1984 election. His campaign manager was the company's president, and his wife was vice president. She negotiated a $2.6 million loan from the co-founder of a company which had extensive dealings with the minister's department. The loan was interest free for the first year. Apparently Mr. Steven's company had been very strapped for cash.

That is the short version of the story. Canadians were expected to believe that Mr. Stevens and his wife never talked about the company or what Mrs. Stevens had been doing to place the company on a less precarious financial footing. It was also mere coincidence that Mr. Stevens personally approved $18.3 million in government grants during the first half of 1985 to a company closely linked to the man who negotiated the loan with his wife.

As usual, the Mulroneyites saw nothing wrong. The government insisted that Mr. Stevens was an honourable man. Finally, on May 12, 1986, when the country couldn't take any more, Stevens resigned from cabinet.

Mr. Justice William Parker was appointed to conduct an inquiry. Mr. Mulroney said he expected his minister to be **"fully vindicated."** In December, 1987, Justice Parker concluded that Mr. Stevens broke conflict rules on 14 occasions while in cabinet and that he showed **"complete disregard"** for the standards of conduct expected of someone holding such high office. What about the blind trust? Mr. Justice Parker found that it **"was not in fact blind,"** something the opposition had been alleging all along. As for Mr. Neilsen, he was dropped from cabinet in June, 1986. The following year he resigned from the House of Commons and was appointed Chairman of the National Transportation Agency.

While the Sinclair Stevens affair was heating up on the conflict of interest side, the Michel Gravel story was beginning to unwind on the corruption front. On May 15, 1986, Mr. Gravel, Conservative MP for Gamelin, was charged with 50 counts of influence peddling, fraud and abuse of public trust.

The charges against Gravel came just hours after a beleaguered Mulroney - stoutly defending his action in the Stevens case - boasted that the Conservatives "are erecting a new standard of morality day by day in Canada." (*Ottawa Citizen,* **May 16/86**)

The Mulroneyites certainly were out to change the standards of political morality in Canada!

It was alleged that Mr. Gravel obtained more than $100,000 in bribes from contractors doing business with the government. Mr. Gravel announced that he was innocent. In the *Montreal Gazette* of April 10, 1986, Public Works Minister Roche LaSalle insisted that **"it is impossible for anyone to influence the awarding of federal contracts"**. As we shall see when we return to the Gravel story, he was proven wrong.

June of 1986 was a particularly big month for the Mulroneyites. On June 9, it was revealed that while on a three-day tour of the western provinces earlier in the year to sell Wilson's budget, Mulroney was accompanied by a seven man video team flying in its own separate Armed Forces Hercules Aircraft. Their job was to film the Life of Brian. Travel cost? - $40,000; plus the salaries of the film crew and the flight crew.

Deputy Prime Minister Erik Nielsen said this was nothing unusual because it was **"a well established practice that goes back to 1978 when it was put in place by Prime Minister Trudeau."** (*Hansard*, June 10/86, p. 14167) Another brassy lie. No previous prime minister had ever been accompanied on his travels by a separate aircraft dedicated to recording his every move for posterity. Neilsen's response, however, was typical — when in trouble, smear the opposition.

The *Globe and Mail* of June 18, 1986, reported:

Prime Minister Brian Mulroney and his entourage spent $811,653.19 on three foreign trips between October and March, including $1,200 a night for a New York hotel suite for the Prime Minister and $830 for a suite for an aide, figures released yesterday show.

Wasn't $1,200 dollars a night for a hotel room just a little steep? No.

Prime Minister Brian Mulroney needs to stay at expensive hotels while abroad because doing so reflects Canada's "standing and pride" in international circles, External Affairs Minister Joe Clark says. (*Toronto Star*, June 19/86)

In fact, $1,200 a night was a bargain compared to the $3,400 a night suite the Mulroneys had booked while in Paris earlier in the year. When he went on that trip to attend the Francophonie Summit, Mr. Mulroney took with him a 54-member entourage which wined and dined one another at working meetings.

They dined on oysters, lamb, goose liver, venison, duck paté and kidneys washed down with champagne and burgundy. (*Montreal Gazette*, June 20/86)

Ah! The hardships of serving Canada abroad.

Everyone got into the act. Lucien Bouchard, a university friend of Mulroney, who had been named as Canada's ambassador to France, put in a bill **"for $67.72 to buy 100 grams of Russian Beluga caviar. The receipt indicates it was for a lunch for Mila Mulroney."** (*Ibid.*)

All those diplomatic functions do get one down, you know. But she still needed recruitment, so

Jocelyne Bouchard, wife of the ambassador, gave a lunch for Mila Mulroney and her "assistant."

The lunch at Bofingers, a well-known Paris eatery, came to $253.52. (*Ibid.*)

To get back and forth from these dinners and luncheons, $109,000 was set aside for a fleet of chauffeur-driven cars. According to the *Montreal Gazette*, even Bonnie Brownlee, press secretary and best friend to Mila Mulroney, had her own car.

The total cost of this week-long trip was more than $520,000. It was later learned that the French Government picked up part of the tab, but confusion remains about exactly how much Canadian taxpayers paid.

A few days later, it was revealed that the government spent $42,000 to celebrate a visit by Mulroney to Washington. A 16-page magazine, with 17 photographs of Mulroney, was published by our embassy for distribution exclusively in the United States. In words and pictures it described the wonderful gala in Washington:

Nancy wore a glittering gown of bronze and gold, Mila one of glowing purple, and the men were wearing tuxedos of unexceptional cut....

They sat at small tables adorned with pink tulips, ate Angel Hair Pasta with Seafood and Romano Cheese Sauce, Supreme of Chicken Vol-au-Vent and Pistachio Marquise, and drank Sonoma-Cutrer Chardonnay, Leardini Pinot Noir and Schramsberg Crémant Demi-Sec. (*Canada Today*, Vol. 17, No. 2, 1986)

On the very day the Mulroneys and Reagans were dining among the tulips, back in Ottawa the Mulroneyites were giving third and

PATRONAGE FROM THE "PINOCCHIO OF POLITICS"

final reading to legislation reducing family allowance payments for even the very poorest children in Canada. No Angel Hair Pasta for them! Thereafter even Kraft Dinner would be harder to buy.

Reports of the Prime Ministers extravagant behaviour surfacing again in August.

National Defence spent nearly $300,000 on a flight that ferried a video film crew recording Prime Minister Brian Mulroney's May tour to Japan, China and South Korea, departmental records show. (*Ottawa Citizen*, Aug. 22/86)

In September Canadians learned that Mulroney took his butler and maid with him on that Asian trip, another first for a Canadian Prime Minister.

The servants' duties included serving meals, pouring tea, and helping the prime minister and his wife to dress, said Mulroney spokesman Marc Lortie. (*Ottawa Citizen*, Sept. 30/86)

Mr. Lortie must have gotten into some hot water with that response, because Mr. Mulroney said it was all a grotesque lie.

"I didn't take a butler. I didn't take anybody," Mulroney said in a CBC interview aired Sunday night.... "I took the people who help us travel." (*Ottawa Citizen*, Oct. 6/86)

If the two individuals, who were the butler and maid at 24 Sussex, were not the butler and maid while travelling with Mulroney in Asia, who then were they and what were they doing? The Solicitor-General of Canada, James Kelleher, had the answer:

"I call them GR-2 employees." Mr. Kelleher said. (*Globe and Mail*, Oct. 7/86)

The butler and the maid had a vital security role.

They were not doing that at all, Mr. Kelleher said. "They were closing the gap. There's outside security and there's inside security." The Khan-Narcisco team were inside security.

When the Prime Minister is "out of his suite, they must remain in his suite at all times, to make sure that unauthori-

zed people don't come in," Mr. Kelleher said. He admitted that the RCMP may be guarding the room as well. (*Ibid*.)

Needless to say, Canadians were fascinated with the story of the butler and maid who double as secret agents on the PM's foreign travels. It was straight out of James Bond, but with the difference that we were expected to believe that fantasy was reality.

In 1986, we learned from the Auditor General of Canada, Kenneth Dye, that the decision to switch the construction of a new federal prison from Drummondville to Mulroney's own riding was going to cost taxpayers $10 million in extra construction costs and another $3 million in additional operating cost every year. Mr. Dye concluded that the prison's construction **"cannot be justified on the basis of need."** (*Montreal Gazette*, Oct. 22/86)

We also learned that three architectural firms that had been awarded a $4.2 million contract by Public Works Minister, Roch LaSalle, to work on the prison were generous contributors to the Progressive Conservative Party.

Jean-Marie Lavoie, said in a telephone interview that his firm always makes larger donations to the party in power. He said local companies have no choice but to attend Tory fund-raising events and make generous donations if they hope to get any Government contracts. (*Globe and Mail***, Oct. 29/86)**

Mr. Lavoie's firm was one of the three doing the prison work. The $4.2 million contract had not been put to public tender.

Let us end 1986 with a story from the *Globe and Mail* of December 16 about Mr. Stephen Walter, who was appointed a citizenship judge by Mr. Mulroney in 1985. Perhaps here we had an appointment that would finally bring honour to all Canadians. The story reads:

A man who applied for citizenship last week said yesterday that Toronto Citizenship Court Judge Stephen Walter told him that he should vote Progressive Conservative in the next election and work for the Tory party.

PATRONAGE FROM THE "PINOCCHIO OF POLITICS"

> Al Roberts, a landed immigrant from India, said Judge Walter told him that voting Liberal would lead Canada "back into socialism and ultimately communism...
>
> [T]he judge began by asking him what he thought of Prime Minister Rajiv Gandhi of India. Mr. Roberts, who has lived in Canada for 7 years, said he had been away from India for some time and could not comment.
>
> The judge then said the Gandhi family was a bunch of "Communist bastards" and that India was a country that leaned to the left....
>
> Mr. Roberts said in his statement that the judge later asked him which Canadian political party he supported. When he replied that he was disappointed with Conservative policy and was leaning toward the Liberals, "the judge totally lost his composure and cast (my) application aside with the comment: 'I am disappointed in you'".
>
> Mr. Roberts said Judge Walter asked him to pick up a framed letter of appreciation from Finance Minister Michael Wilson and read it.
>
> "Meanwhile, he lectured (me) on the good the Conservatives had done and about his association with people like Michael Wilson and Brian Mulroney.
>
> "He called (me) and the Liberal Party socialists. He said I should not only vote Conservative but also work for the party."

Following similar stories from others who appeared before him, Judge Walter decided that he had brought enough "honour to Canada" and resigned. In his letter of resignation, he said he was **"deeply saddened"** that the media coverage **"appears to have brought embarrassment to the Government which I was so proud to serve."** (*Globe and Mail*, December 19/86)

The next two years followed the pattern established in 1985 and 1986. 1987 began with another cabinet resignation. This time it was Andre Bissonnette, Secretary of State for Transport. Oerlikon Aerospace Inc., a weapon's manufacturer, had decided to build a plant in Bissonnette's riding in anticipation of landing a lucrative government contract. It paid $2.98 million for vacant farmland that had been sold eleven days earlier for $800,000. During that eleven-day interval, Normand Ouellette, Bissonnette's childhood friend, business associate, political organizer, riding president and business trustee, bought the land and resold it to Oerlikon for a $920,000 profit. He then invested that profit in term deposits on behalf of two of his own companies and two companies owned by Mr. and Mrs. Bissonnette. Both men were charged with fraud and bribery. The former minister was acquitted while his riding association president was convicted. Mr. Ouellette was fined $100,000 and ordered to reimburse the Oerlikon Company more than $1 million.

In 1987 and 1988, there was more political corruption, including the gangland-style murder of a Tory fundraiser who was linked to questionable land transactions around Mirabel Airport. Canadians saw accusations made by former Mulroney minister Suzanne Blais-Grenier that companies dealing with the federal government routinely gave kickbacks in order to secure contracts: **"I'm not talking about $500 under the table or $1,000 in someone's pocket, I'm talking about millions of dollars,"** she said. (*Globe and Mail*, Aug. 24/88)

In addition to corruption, there was more patronage, conflict of interest, and plain greed. The Supply and Services Minister, Michel Cote, was fired early in 1988, after it was revealed that he failed to report, as required by conflict of interest guidelines, a personal loan of $250,000 from a businessman whose company had dealings with the federal government.

Perhaps Mr. Richard Cleroux has even more we could look at, but as a finale, let's turn to one of the highlights of 1987, namely, Guccigate. On April 16, 1987, the *Globe and Mail* reported how the Mulroneys went redecoration crazy after moving into 24 Sussex Drive. After spending the almost $100,000 available in public funds, Mr. Mulroney turned to his party for another $308,000. The money was used for things such as a clothes closet for Mr. Mulroney, **"designed to accommodate 30 suits and 84 pairs of shoes, including at least 50 pairs of Gucci loafers."** Mrs. Mulroney had a closet constructed that could provide storage for 100 pairs of shoes. Many eyebrows were raised at the revelation that tax deductible contributions to the Conservative party were being used to help the Mulroney's emulate the lifestyle made famous by Imelda Marcos. Why are dozens of pairs of shoes the outward and visible sign of First-Lady status?

Canadians were told not to worry. In fact, they should be grateful. PC Canada Fund chairman, David Angus explained that the PM had paid back $158,000 of the money.

Mr. Angus said the PC Canada Fund owns about $150,000 worth of furnishings in the official residences and that Mr. Mulroney owns the rest, which are worth about $158,000. (*Globe and Mail*, Apr. 17/87)

What was going to happen to the furnishings owned by the Party?

Mr. Lortie Mulroney's press secretary indicated yesterday that the Tories might decide to give their share of the furnishings to the Crown, "so they will be to the benefit of the prime ministers. Or they may be given to a museum." (*Ibid.*)

An anonymous Tory fundraiser comment: **"This furniture is going to be a generous gift to the country.... What are we going to do when Mulroney leaves? Have a garage sale outside Sussex Drive?"** (*Ottawa Citizen*, Apr. 25/87) In a manner of speaking, Yes. There was a garage sale in 1993 but it was held inside 24 Sussex Drive and there was only one customer, the Government of Canada.

We now know that Mrs. Mulroney, in the dying days of her husband's administration, struck a deal with the government to purchase her surplus carpets, furniture and clothes closet for $150,000. Prime Minister Kim Campbell was pleased with the arrangement: **"It seems to me to be a bit of a bargain,"** she said (Ottawa Citizen, July 2/93). No longer was there any talk of giving the furnishings to the people of Canada. Those in the know refused to discuss where the furniture had come from or who had paid for it. For instance, what had become of the $150,000 of furnishings owned by the PC Canada Fund?

THE SHOW MUST NOT GO ON

"The PC Fund has nothing to do with any of this stuff," (David) Angus said Thursday evening. "That's all I have to say." (*Ottawa Citizen*, July 2/93)

According to the *Globe and Mail* of July 9, 1993, **"The party now says it has no proprietary interest in any of the furnishings at the residences."** The furnishings owned by the Conservative Party had apparently vanished.

In response to the public outcry, Mrs. Mulroney cancelled the $150,000 sale, and expressed mystification at the public's reaction to her noble motives:

"I am of course disappointed by the suggestion — even from some partisan sources — that I might have sought to profit from this transaction."

She had acted **"in the genuine belief that such an initiative would benefit the Canadian taxpayer and lessen the burden on future prime ministers. I regret this gesture was misconstrued."** (*Globe and Mail*, July 16/93)

As we close this chapter, let's return to where we started, with the statement by Richard Cleroux.

"We here in Canada between 1984 and 1992 have lived through the most corruption-ridden federal government in our history."

Is there evidence to support his charge? It seems so. And even more evidence surfaced after the 1988 election.

10.

"HONEST" BRIAN V. "TRAITOR" JOHN — ELECTION '88

EVERYTHING THE MULRONEYITES DID IN 1988 was done with a view to the forthcoming election. The overriding priority was to induce a collective state of amnesia across the country. Canadians had to forget that the performance of the team bore no relationship — certainly no positive relationship — to what had been promised. They had to forget about all the broken promises. That was the strategy. The tactics were simple: first, say whatever it takes to win the election, even if it means showing a total disregard for the truth; and, second, tar and smear the opposition as liars, especially when they are telling the truth. Just as in 1984, it was to be a campaign of spin and distortion.

For the Mulroney Conservative team, the 1988 election campaign began with Michael Wilson's budget of February 10, 1988. As we have seen, in 1984 the deficit wasn't a major concern. In 1985, it became a priority. In 1986, a call to arms. In 1987, the deficit was under control, and in 1988, Mr. Wilson announced that it had been caged and tamed. In his budget speech, the Finance Minister announced: **"We have restored fiscal responsibility by reducing the deficit and cutting the growth of the national debt."**

In the 1988 budget, Mr. Wilson's tough deficit talk had disappeared. John Ferguson, of the *Montreal Gazette*, began his February 11, 1988, column:

> **The Chinese have an expression which best sums up Michael Wilson's budget: "Big noise at top of stairs, no one comes down."**

Although the deficit still stood at approximately $29 billion, only $3 billion less than in 1983-84, the last complete Liberal fiscal year, the battle was suddenly over and victory was declared. A headline in the *Globe and Mail* of February 11, had it right: "**Attack on deficit takes back seat to Tory programs.**"

Instead of a battle against the deficit, new programs were announced months before the general election call. In June of 1988, Mulroney's friend and confidant, Lucien Bouchard, was seeking entry into the House of Commons via a by-election in the riding of Lac Saint-Jean. Never one to deny help to a friend in need, Mr. Mulroney bravely confronted the task of getting Bouchard elected. He threw money at the problem.

The *Montreal Gazette*, June 14, 1988, described how Mulroney suggested there might be $40 million in federal funds to help construct a highway between Lac Saint-Jean and James Bay.

> "These aren't presents I'm talking about," he continued. "A road for a remote region isn't a present. It's an investment.... It's an investment in your future."

Two days later the *Montreal Gazette* reported how Mr. Mulroney personally approved a $1.5 million grant to a job creation centre in the riding. This grant was approved within days of the request, as opposed to the 6 to 8 weeks it normally took to process such grants. There was more, including half-a-billion dollars in federal money for regional development in the province.

Mr. Bouchard won the election, but a few years later used it and his resultant national prominance as a springboard to launch his separatist Bloc Québécois.

In addition to these specific promises on behalf of a dear friend, there were promises designed to appeal much more widely. The *Globe and Mail* of August 15, reported how Mr. Mulroney suggested there might be federal money for the construction of a $1 billion aluminium smelter in Sept-Iles. There were promises of $1 billion to develop Hibernia, with another $1.6 billion in loan guarantees. There was $420 million for all-terrain vehicles for the Armed Forces. There was $150 million promised for a natural gas pipeline to Vancouver Island; $400 million for the Husky heavy oil upgrader in Lloydminster; $110 million to fight illiteracy; $88 million for grape-growers; $1 billion for the OSLO oils sands project; $250 million for the Canadian film industry; $39 million to combat family violence; $165 million for western drought relief; $129 for AIDS research; and an extra $1 billion for child care. As the *Globe and Mail* of June 11, 1988, reported:

> **With military-like precision, Government corporate jets carrying Cabinet ministers have been dispatched daily on missions from coast to coast, distributing money to often unsuspecting citizens.**

According to the October 5, 1988, edition of the *Toronto Star*, it amounted to **"a $16 billion pre-election spending spree."**

When the election was called, Mr. Mulroney immediately showed that he was fully prepared to shatter the record he had established for cynicism during the 1984 campaign. As everyone knows, the Prime Minister had long been making promises about a national child care program. His government finally acted in 1988. On Tuesday, September 27, 1988, Bill C-144, the child care bill, after having cleared the House of Commons, arrived in the Senate and was given first reading. Under the rules of the Senate, debate on 2nd reading could not start until two days later. Liberal Senators, however, agreed to waive the rule and debate began that same afternoon. The next day, on Wednesday, September 28, the bill was given 2nd reading and referred to a committee.

Was the Prime Minister grateful that his bill was advancing so rapidly in Senate? Was he pleased that the Opposition was waiving the normal rules in order to get it into committee within 24 hours of receipt? The answer is No.

In a CBC interview aired on September 28, Mr. Mulroney said **"what the Senate has done is already obstructive"**. He claimed that **"working women need these spaces tomorrow"** and that they were **"suffering substantially"** because of the Senate's actions. The hypocrisy was breathtaking.

The Senate committee quickly started its work and began holding hearings. It was interesting that virtually the entire day care community opposed the bill, believing that more federal funding would be available under existing Canada Assistance Plan provisions. Nevertheless, as the rhetoric from the Prime Minister escalated, the Senate Opposition Leader, Allan MacEachen, on Friday, September 30, countered with the following statement,

> **"We are prepared to have the committee continue its work tomorrow, with a view to affording the committee enough time to report the bill tomorrow. We are prepared to have the consideration of that report completed in the Senate and, indeed, have Royal Assent tomorrow at some point, depending upon the progress that is made in committee."** (*Debates*, p. 4550)

There was the offer. Passage and royal assent of the bill before the end of the following day. No one on the government benches said a word in reply. Nothing from the government leader, Senator Murray. Not a word from the deputy government leader, Senator William Doody. Not a word from the government whip, Senator Orville Phillips. The reason for their silence became painfully obvious the next day.

The whole thing was a shameful and cynical set-up. On the morning of Saturday, October 1, the committee met in order to hear the final witnesses and to prepare its report. In the middle of the hearings, Senator Phillips stormed into the committee room and declared that the committee had no right to meet any longer because Parliament had just been dissolved by the Governor General at the request of the Prime Minister. There was to be an election. All legislation still before Parliament, including the child care bill, died with the election call.

Could Mulroney not have accepted Senator MacEachen's offer and delayed the dissolution of Parliament until Bill C-144 had become law later that day? We are not talking about days, just later that same day. If he had done so, he would have ensured passage of the legislation that, to use his own words, working women who were "suffering substantially" so badly needed. The answer is No, he could not wait because he never really wanted the bill to become law. So he called the election and killed Bill C-144.

A mere three days into the campaign, after yanking the rug out from under his own bill, Mulroney's attacks on the Senate began. The *London Free Press* of Tuesday, October 4, 1988, reported:

"HONEST" BRIAN V. "TRAITOR" JOHN

> The prime minister said Senate Liberal leader Allan MacEachen and fellow Liberal senators "killed" his child-care legislation by stalling it in the Senate last month.

Is there some kind of penance Mr. Mulroney does after making statements like this? Apparently not because he keeps making them, including as recently as April 27, 1993. At pages 18530-1 of *Hansard*, Mr. Mulroney is shown responding to a charge that he broke his promise of a national day care program:

> "Mr. Speaker, my hon. friend is indulging in revisionism. This House passed a national child care program in 1988 and it was killed in the Senate by the Liberal Party.
>
> ... it was killed by the Liberals led by the Hon. Allan MacEachen in the Senate. The Liberal Party of Canada killed a national child care program and you will pay for it forever."

After pulling the plug on his own day care legislation, Mr. Mulroney promised it all over again during the election campaign, and then promptly broke his promise when safely back at 24 Sussex Drive.

During the campaign, Mr. Mulroney was careful to follow faithfully previously successful tactics of deception and smear. The *Globe and Mail* of October 10, 1988, reports how he told North Shore residents: **"we have kept our promises."** From the same newspaper, dated October 17, 1988, there is a report of another Mulroney promise in Prince Edward Island.

> "Let me say a special word to senior citizens: in the future Canada will be doing more, not less for all of you," he told about 100 seniors at the Parkview Senior Citizens Club in Summerside on Saturday morning....
>
> "As long as I am Prime Minister of Canada, social benefits — especially those for the elderly — will be improved, not diminished by the government, which is committed to social justice and fairness for all Canadians".

During the leaders' debate he repeated his assurances.

How did Mr. Mulroney keep his promise of improving, not diminishing social benefits for seniors? Immediately following the election, he introduced the claw-back, and tens of thousands of seniors saw their old age pension money disappear.

As the election race tightened, the Mulroneyites turned more and more to smear tactics. Mulroney accused John Turner and Ed Broadbent of being **"shameful and dishonest"** about their statements on the free trade deal. (*Toronto Star*, October 28) Then Michael Wilson joined the fray. According to the *Toronto Star* of November 1, 1988, Mr. Wilson said in an Ottawa speech: **"to sow fear and peddle lies is much easier than to build a country."** Responding to Turner's charge that free trade imperilled our social programs, he said: **"I say to Mr. Turner that this is a lie."** It must be ironic and difficult for Mr. Turner to think back about being called a liar for saying things that soon turned out to be right.

The *Ottawa Citizen* of November 2, 1988, describes how Mr. Mulroney took up the chant of his Finance Minister, saying:

> **"They should tell the truth, not sow fear among the elderly, not sow fear among the poor...."**

Next, it was the turn of Deputy Prime Minister, Don Mazankowski. The first paragraph of a November 2, Toronto Star article reads:

> **It's time for a government truth squad to expose the "big lie" being told by opposition parties on free trade, Deputy Prime Minister Don Mazankowski says.**

According to the *Toronto Star* of November 3, 1988, Mr. Mulroney charged that the lies of his opponents had become so outrageous that:

> **"They owe Canadians, especially senior citizens, an immediate and genuine retraction and apology....**
>
> **The Opposition parties thought they could get through an election campaign propagating deception and distortion and deceit. I think that the opposition parties believed that a lie that goes unchallenged for 24 hours would automatically become the truth."**

"HONEST" BRIAN V. "TRAITOR" JOHN

The *Globe and Mail* of November 3, reported that John Crosbie also charged Liberals of spreading **"deliberate lies and untruths."** The party line was set and the team members were fanning out across the country delivering it.

The *Ottawa Citizen* of the same day reported how Mr. Crosbie had claimed that the Economic Council of Canada believed that rejection of the FTA would lead to a flight of capital out of Canada. However, the article continued with the observation that the council said no such thing.

The *Toronto Star* of November 4, described a visit Mr. Mulroney paid to a senior citizens home in Edmonton:

> **In a grave voice, Mulroney gave them his best prime ministerial assurance: "No one is going to take away your pensions or medical services."**

As we have seen, that was a lie.

When retired Supreme Court Justice Emmet Hall offered the opinion that free trade did not endanger medicare, Mr. Mulroney reached the pinnacle of his smear campaign against John Turner. As the *Ottawa Citizen* of November 5, reported:

> **The 89-year-old Hall came forward "to nail the lies down and to pin them right on John Turner's forehead," Mulroney said.**

He was right about the lies, although he had the wrong forehead. Conservative television ads repeated the same Tory message.

> **"John Turner says there's something in the free-trade agreement that threatens Canada's sovereignty," says an announcer's voice, as the map of North America shows on the screen.**
>
> **"That's a lie," the voice continues...** (*Ottawa Citizen*, Nov. 7/88)

On November 15, Simon Reisman was brought in as the clean-up hitter. He said:

> **"I think the man who is selling out Canada is John Turner because he's reckless, he's betraying the country and he's playing with the future of our children and grandchildren...I**

challenge him, I accuse him of being a traitor to Canada for saying the things he is saying." (*Ottawa Citizen,* Nov. 15/88)

A fomer civil servant, wades in on behalf of the Mulroneyites, and accuses the former Prime Minister of Canada of being a traitor. Worth remembering how far this gang will go when they feel cornered. Mr. Reisman showed how far the Mulroney team was willing to go in smearing a political opponent and no member of Mulroney's cabinet publicly rebuked Reisman's foolishness.

Turner, unwilling to join Mulroney in the gutter, paid the electoral price.

That was the smear portion of the campaign. The other part was to say anything so long as it led to electoral success. Already we have seen some good examples from the team leader himself, including promises to seniors and working mothers. But the master of the art of deception during the 1988 campaign was finance minister Michael Wilson, the same Mr. Wilson who in 1993 so ardently embraces Ms. Kim Campbell as a kindred spirit, because she is going to continue his policies, we are told. First, Wilson attacked the Liberal campaign platform.

> "All I know, having been Finance Minister for the past four years, is John Turner is going to have to break those promises or we're going to have taxes going sky-high or the deficit going sky-high." (*Globe and Mail,* Nov. 3/88)

What about the Conservative promises? Mr. Wilson knew of none, according to the *Globe and Mail* of November 11:

> **The Progressive Conservative Party has not made any election promises during this campaign, Finance Minister Michael Wilson said in an extraordinary exchange with reporters last night.**
>
> **Liberals, he said, have made election spending promises. Conservatives have made "spending commitments."**
>
> **According to Mr. Wilson, the current election-promise score in this campaign is $37.7 billion for the Liberals to zero for the Conservatives.**

"In the way that I've described it, yes, it's zero," he said.

If they were not promises, but so-called "spending commitments," would they be kept by a Conservative government?

"Forget there's an election," Mr. Wilson added. He said that all Tory promises could be covered by the flexibility written into the five-year "spending track."

Remember those words - **"Forget there's an election"**. Mr. Wilson continued:

"In those reserves, we have sufficient money to handle the announcements that we made prior to the election and those that have been made since the election was called."

Late in the campaign, there were rumours that rising interest rates were pushing up the deficit. Wood Gundy Inc. released a study warning:

"...with interest rates already over 200 basis points higher than forecast in the current fiscal plan, the government's estimate of a $28.6-billion deficit for 1989-90 is simply unobtainable in the context of current tax and expenditures policies."

It estimates that in the absence of changes in expenditure policy, Ottawa's budget deficit next year will soar to $32-billion. (*Globe and Mail,* **Nov. 15/88**)

The article disclosed that even some government sources were confidentially predicting the same scenarios. What did the Mulroneyites do? They simply called Wood Gundy liars, like anyone else they found troublesome. Mr. Wilson's response is found in the *Ottawa Citizen* of November 15, 1988.

A report that the government now expects the deficit to rise to $32 billion next year is wrong, Finance Minister Wilson said Monday.

"No, that's not accurate," Wilson said as he left a Conservative rally at which Prime Minister Brian Mulroney spoke to about 3,000 business supporters.

THE SHOW MUST NOT GO ON

Mulroney refused to answer any questions on the report as he left the rally

... "I don't know the basis on which anybody is making those assumptions," Wilson said, adding "I don't buy those assumptions."

"I made it very clear that our program spending track is right on line," he said.

But it was not on track. Following the election, Mr. Wilson all but admitted that he had been less than truthful during the campaign. He announced that higher interest rates had pushed up public debt charges for the 1989/90 fiscal year by $6.4 billion. That was twice as high as even Wood Gundy had been predicting.

Did Mr. Wilson apologize for misleading Canadians and for calling Wood Gundy "Liars". Of course he didn't. Instead, he hammered Canadians with higher taxes, cancelled wholesale the election promises — sorry, "commitments" — and launched his most determined assault yet on our social programs.

Perhaps a new maxim seems to be emerging: anyone called a liar by this gang probably is telling the truth.

During the election Wilson had said to Canadians **"Forget there's an election."** Now he was telling Canadians "Forget there was an election and forget everything I said during the election." He should have added, "Forget also anything my team members said and everything the Prime Minister said."

For the Mulroney team, however, the important thing was that the election had been won. The Mulroneyites, including Kim Campbell, marched into office with no qualms about doing the exact opposite of what they had promised. As in 1984, there were no apologies for misleading Canadians. Far from it. At the Tory leadership convention early in 1993, Mulroney declared **"We kept our word,"** a sure sign of what to expect in Election '93.

In retrospect, the only words Mulroney kept were those he uttered during the Throne Speech debate on November 7, 1984, when he said: **"Give us 20 years ... and you will not recognize this country."**

And it only took nine years, not 20.

11.

"FORGET THERE WAS AN ELECTION" AND EVERYTHING WE SAID

THE FIRST ORDER OF BUSINESS for the Mulroneyites following the election was passage into law of the free trade agreement with the United States. That was done on December 30, 1988.

The second was to make the billions of dollars of campaign promises disappear. That was done by Michael Wilson in his budget of April 26, 1989. But Wilson could not do it alone. He turned to his corporate friends and they obligingly set the stage.

During the election campaign, the Canadians business community spent millions of dollars touting the Free Trade Agreement. They advertised individually and as members of an umbrella group called "The Canadian Alliance for Trade and Job Opportunities." In full-page newspaper ads members of the Alliance claimed that **"Free Trade means more prosperity...more employment, more pension money, more money for social services...."** (*Toronto Star*, Nov. 16/88) In a four page insert distributed with the *Globe and Mail* and other newspapers on November 3, 1988, the Alliance assured Canadians, in a question and answer format, that their social programs would not only be maintained, but expanded.

> *Question:* **So what's in it for me?**
>
> *Answer:* **More jobs. Better Jobs. More wealth to improve government services such as daycare....**
>
> *Question:* **But won't the agreement gradually force us to align our policies along the lines of the larger and stronger partner? Won't Canadian business lobby to reduce spending on social and other programs?**
>
> *Answer:* **Not at all.**

Of course they wouldn't. Less than four months later, with the Free Trade Agreement safely passed into law, the business community, emulating Michael Wilson, was urging Canadians to forget there had been election and to forget everything that had been said.

> **Social programs must be slashed and more tax breaks given to business if Canada is to remain competitive under the free-trade agreement, a major business lobby said Tuesday.**
>
> **... the Canadian Manufacturers Association claimed Canadian competitiveness with U.S. firms is handicapped by the "critical" debt. The burden of deficit reduction must fall on spending cuts, especially on social programs.** (*Ottawa Citizen*, Mar. 1/89)

Then Thomas d'Aquino, president of the Business Council on National Issues took up the new line. He had been the most vocal and visible business supporter of the FTA during the election campaign and a driving force behind The Canadian Alliance for Trade and Job Opportunities. Now he warned that the national debt **"is a voracious monster and into its gaping maw goes a higher and higher proportion of our tax dollars."** (*Ottawa Citizen*, Mar. 1/89) His solution was to slash government expenditures. **"Canada's elaborate system of income support programs cannot be exempted from a comprehensive deficit-reduction strategy,"** he said. (*Ottawa Citizen*, Mar. 10/89)

The Canadian Chamber of Commerce spoke next. It declared that **"all Canadians should be extremely concerned about the deficit/debt problem"** and called for an **"austerity program."** (*Press Release*, Mar. 2/89)

Corporate lawyers took up the cry with zealous fervour:

> **"The rapidly growing national debt puts Canada's future in jeopardy...Canada...faces a crisis."** (W.A. Macdonald, *Globe and Mail*, Apr. 6/89)

Mr. Macdonald asked Canadians to **"search their souls."**

Then, the press joined in. The *Ottawa Citizen* of Saturday, April 8, 1989, contained a special 12-page feature on the deficit. The headline, in blood red ink, was **"Our Crushing Deficit."** The letters were almost 4 inches high, a size normally reserved for declarations of war. Underneath was a stylized drawing of a man being forced to his knees by the crushing weight of the yoke of debt piled on his shoulders. There was not a single advertisement to interfere with stories headlined **"When a country goes broke, the result can be CHAOS"**, and **"The auctioning off of Canada"**.

With the stage thus set, Mr. Michael Wilson strides forth on April 10, 1989, to declare, in a speech to the Retail Council of Canada, that the country faced **"one overarching problem. That problem is the growing size of the public debt and the exploding cost of paying interest on that debt."**

And Canadians bought the new, post-election line. According to an Angus Reid Poll,

> **The proportion of Canadians who now see the deficit as the major problem facing the country has nearly doubled from January and is more than four times greater than during the election campaign last fall. (*Globe and Mail*, Apr. 17/89)**

Remember what Canadians were told before the election? Remember how Mr. Wilson had said, **"our program spending track is right on line"**? A week before election day, he was telling Canadians that he had **"reserves"**. Now he was broke. Well, the final step in the repudiation of the entire election campaign took place on April 16, 1989, when Michael Wilson prematurely released his leaked budget in a televised press conference. He revealed that **"the most important challenge"** facing Canadians was **"our large and growing public debt."** (*Budget Speech*, p. 1) He admitted what he had categorically denied one week before election day, namely, that rising interest rates had knocked his deficit projections right out the window.

> **Short-term interest rate are now expected to be more than 4 percentage points higher on average in 1989 than was projected in the February 1988 budget. These higher interest rates have put upward pressure on the deficit. (*The Fiscal Plan*, p. 10-11)**

For the 1989-90 fiscal year, it was $6.4 billion worth of pressure. It was time to tax and slash. His so-called spending "commitments" were now to be treated no differently than ordinary Tory promises — made to be broken.

What had happened to his "reserves" that were going to cover all the promises he and his leader had made? What about his categorical denials when Wood Gundy Inc. said that rising interest rates had already pushed up the deficit by more than $3 billion? Remember how he said **"No, that's not accurate"**, and **"I don't buy those assumptions"**!

Well, the *Ottawa Citizen* applied, under the Freedom of Information Act, for the economic forecasts his department had provided him during the election campaign. Mr. Wilson refused to release them. Information Commissioner, Inger Hansen, demanded that he provide them. Again he refused. Instead of providing the forecasts, he dumped a

> **six-inch pile of essays on matters such as "The Impact of the Drought on the U.S. Economy" on the *Citizen* and pretended they were, in fact, what was being sought. (*Ottawa Citizen*, Oct. 13/89)**

The *Ottawa Citizen* never did get the forecasts and Canadians never did find out what Mr. Wilson knew when he assured them everything was on track. Instead of facts, they got more taxes and more cuts.

First, the tax increases. The so-called "temporary" personal income surtax was increased by two percentage points and a new surtax of 3 per cent was imposed on higher-income taxpayers. The excise tax on cigarettes and gasoline was increased. The federal sales tax was increased from 12% to 13%. Unemployment insurance premiums were increased, as were some corporate taxes.

Then the social programs, old age security pensions and family allowances were clawed back from individuals earning more than $50,000. Hundreds of thousands of families were affected. So much for Mr. Mulroney's personal pledge to seniors in Edmonton that, **"No one is going to take away your pensions."** He made this promise with touching sincerity. Then with the help of Wilson and the Tory ministers he clawed at their pensions and took them away.

In his budget, Mr. Wilson announced also that the government would no longer contribute to the Unemployment Insurance Fund and that the growth of transfers to the provinces for health care and education was to be cut.

Our foreign aid assistance, including food aid for the truly impoverished, was cut.

VIA rail subsidies were cut, as was National Defence spending.

There were cuts to programs for natives and women, as well for cooperative housing, the publishing industry, and the CBC.

New programs promised during the election campaign, such as the national day care program, were put on hold or scrapped.

The multibillion dollar nuclear submarine program was also scrapped, probably the only good news in the entire budget.

Even after $3.3 billion in new taxes and $1.5 billion in cuts, the deficit for 1989-90 was projected at $30.5 billion. One couldn't call this progress, but Mr. Wilson urged Canadians to look to the long term: the deficit for the 1993/94 fiscal year would be only $15.0 billion he assured them. Really? He was off by almost $20 billion.

The Mulroneyites could not have been surprised when polls showed that 66% of Canadians regarded the budget as unfair. (Montreal Gazette, May 3/89) But who cared? This was early 1989, and the next election wouldn't come for over four years.

The magnitude of Mr. Wilson's failure became evident the following year when, on February 20, 1990, he delivered his next budget. He proudly announced that there were no new tax increases. But he neglected to mention that in 1990, Canadians would pay $2.1 billion more in new taxes announced in his previous budget. And, following form, there were more cutbacks to transfer payments to the provinces for health care and education. They would amount to $7.3 billion over 5 years. How were the provinces going to make up the difference unless they increased their own taxes to the same taxpayers?

Also the growth of transfer payments for social assistance and daycare to British Columbia, Alberta, and Ontario was limited.

THE SHOW MUST NOT GO ON

Forget about a national day-care program. Not only would there not be one, but existing commitments for federal day-care funding through the Canada Assistance Plan would be cut.

There was to be less money than originally planned for social housing, Indian and Inuit programs, R&D, the CBC and Marine Atlantic. Even the funds to provide shelters for battered women were cut off. The Polar 8 Icebreaker project was cancelled, notwithstanding Mulroney's earlier vow that it would go ahead. He had said that the vessel:

"was a very important instrument for the assertion of sovereignty in Northern Canada." (*Globe and Mail*, May 9/89)

Canadian sovereignty in the north had become a back burner item.

Mr. Wilson predicted a $28.5 billion deficit for the 1990-91 fiscal year. It would come in at $30.5 billion. He predicted a $14 billion deficit for 1993-94. Wrong, more than 100% wrong! He predicted slow but steady growth in the economy. Wrong again. The economy plunged into a home-made recession. The Mulroneyites bragged about their achievements, and now, Mr. Wilson brags that Ms. Campbell will carry where he left off.

After hearing Wilson's 1989 budget, Campbell said she was **"struck by how responsible and responsive this Budget in fact is."** Wilson had been **"both fair and even-handed."** (*Hansard*, May 9/89, p. 1474) She boasted about all the fine work the team had done in fighting the deficit. She confidently predicted that **"The Budget measures will cut the annual deficit in half by $15 billion by 1993-94."** (p. 1473) Now she's taking over being wrong — like Mr. Wilson, she wasn't even close. And she also predicted that **"by the 1990's we will be facing serious labour shortages."** (p. 1472) Wrong again. As we near the end of 1993, more than one-and-a-half million Canadians are facing serious employment shortages. They have no jobs!

How did Ms. Campbell feel about the wholesale abandonment of her party's election promises? Well, she explained that her government's decision not to go ahead with a national daycare program was taken **"with a considerable amount of regret.... How-**

ever, today's demands are very small compared to the demands that we will see 10 years or 20 years down the road...."** (*Hansard*, p. 1472) No help at all for the hundreds of thousands of families seeking day-care for their children. As for the day-care legislation that died with the election call, she said it **"was not acted on by the Senate."** (p. 1475) Absolutely false. We already have seen that it was on the verge of becoming law when Mr. Mulroney pulled the plug on Parliament, thus killing the day-care bill. She had learned from her cabinet colleagues that it is easier to confuse than to explain and defend the facts. No wonder that Mr. Mulroney regards her as his best pupil.

But back to the dreary tale of Finance Minister Michael Wilson. After having helped lead the country into recession, it was time to produce another budget and to break more promises.

Mr. Wilson claimed his February 26, 1991 budget set **"out a Plan for Economic Recovery - a strong confident recovery"** that would lead to **"growth and renewed prosperity."** (*The Budget*, p.2) Wrong again. The recession deepened and the deficit ballooned. Wilson's budget was followed by eight straight months of negative economic growth.

The first promise Mr. Wilson now broke was one he made in his 1989 budget concerning Unemployment Insurance Premiums.

The government will continue to contribute to the financing of the program in difficult economic times when it is inappropriate to raise premiums... To provide for stability in the future... the premium rate for employees will be set at $2.25 per $100 of insurable earnings for 1990, 1991 and 1992." (*The Fiscal Plan*, 1989, p. 34)

He must have concluded that the middle of a recession did not constitute "difficult times" because he broke his promise of a 3-year freeze and raised premiums by 24%! This would pull billions of dollars out of the pockets of workers — $2 billion in 1991/92 and $2.4 billion in 1992/93.

In the House of Commons, a Liberal member, Warren Allmand, asked Mr. Wilson directly: **"Was the minister totally incompetent** when he made that legislative commitment... or was he simply lying to the Canadian people?"** *(Hansard,* Mar. 1/91, p. 17847)

Mr. Wilson had no answer. He left it to his cabinet colleague, Barbara McDougall, to respond. In typical Mulroneyite fashion, she called the question - not the breaking of the promise - "offensive," and attacked the Liberal Party for failing to cooperate with the government's tax and slash agenda. Mr. Wilson sat silent.

The other major tax increase Mr. Wilson announced in his 1991 Budget was on tobacco. It would raise an additional $1 billion a year.

People Programs? As usual, there were more cuts. There were cuts to environmental funding, a $100 million cut to job training — so much for the massive training program promised repeatedly by Mulroney — more cuts to transfers to the provinces and to the public service. Public service wage increases would be held to 3%.

Then Canadians learned that on the very last day before the budget, the Mulroney team had awarded nearly 50 top executives a 4.2% wage increase, retroactive to June 1, 1990. And it couldn't be passed off as a catch-up. Since 1987, the Governor of the Bank of Canada, John Crow, had seen his salary range of $120,000 - $150,000 increase to $168,800 - $253,000. Now he was getting a 4.2% increase while secretaries earning $25,000 were told they would have to make do with 3% or less.

Later in 1991 it was revealed that top bureaucrats were going to get bonuses in the tens of thousands of dollars. The president of CN Rail, for example, already earning more than $300,000, was getting a bonus of at least $30,000.

"They get that ever year," Treasury Board President Gilles Loiselle told the Sun. "We are doing that to get better productivity." *(Ottawa Sun,* **Sept. 26/91)**

The top executives needed carrots to increase their productivity. The workers got the stick. Ms. Campbell must have liked Mr. Loiselle's style because upon being sworn in as Prime Minister, she had made him Minister of Finance.

But back to 1991 and Michael Wilson. His $3.4 billion in new taxes and $1.2 billion in cuts would still result in a higher deficit than the year before. For the 1991-92 fiscal year, he predicted a deficit of $30.5 billion. Predictably, he was wrong: it came in almost $1 billion higher, at $31.4 billion. Not to worry. The real fruits of his wise policies would be borne in subsequent years, he again told Canadians. He predicted that the deficit for 1993-94 would be $16.6 billion. He was spectacularly wrong: the deficit will be twice that high in 1993-94.

Fortunately for Canadians, Mr. Wilson's 1991 budget was his last. Unfortunately, he was sent by Mulroney to work his magic in the NAFTA talks with Mexico and the United States.

What had Michael Wilson accomplished in his seven years as Finance Minister? Why not judge him in terms of his own expectations.

On May 4, 1983, while in opposition, Mr. Wilson gave a speech to the Toronto Stock Exchange, explaining how he would do things.

"Let me give you my prescription....First we must lower taxes."

He lowered them by introducing 40 different tax increases, plus the GST. He continued: **"We can eliminate the deficit within five years...It isn't as hard as it seems."** (*Vancouver Sun*, Oct. 17/90)

That was 10 years ago. That was $275 billion of debt ago. Today, Ms. Campbell says she will eliminate the deficit in five years. New tory; same story.

What was Mr. Mulroney's assessment of Michael Wilson's tenure? Never one to spare the melted butter, he poured it on: **"he is the finest/best finance minister this country/the world has ever seen"**. (*Globe and Mail*, Apr. 22/91) Best? He left with virtually the same deficit he started with, notwithstanding record tax increases and the dismantling of our social programs.

Were even Bay Street and Wall Street happy with his false forecasts and deficits?

Mulroney picked Don Mazankowski as Wilson's successor.

In his budget of February 25, 1992, Mr. Mazankowski reduced some taxes, like the personal income surtax and corporate taxes, and turned on government spending by eliminating agencies such as the Science Council of Canada and the Economic Council of

Canada. This approach, he claimed, would **"keep Canada firmly on course for better times ahead."** (*Budget*, p. 1) Now it was his turn to be wrong.

The economic growth of 2.7% he predicted for 1992 turned out to be only 1%. In only three of the last 30 years had GDP growth been lower, and two of those years had been Wilson's last two!

Mazankowski's projected deficit for the 1992-93 fiscal year of $27.5 billion was so far off track that he had to bring in an *Economic Statement* on December 2, 1992. In that statement, after announcing some more slashes, including cuts to unemployment insurance benefits, he proudly stated that for the 1992-93 fiscal year, **"The actions I have announced today will bring the estimated deficit down to $34.4 billion".** (p. 12) Down? It was supposed to be $27.5 billion. Now Mr. Mazankowski was getting it **"down to $34.4 billion."**

Mr. Mazankowski's next budget, his last, presented on April 26, 1993, was a pamphlet-sized admission of 9 years of depressing failure.

In 1988, Wilson predicted that the deficit for 1992-93 would be $19.5 billion. In 1991, he revised that estimate to $24 billion. In February 1992 Mazankowski said it would be $27.5 billion. Ten months later, another revision, this time up to $34.5 billion. Then, in February 1993, Mazankowski admitted that it would come in at $35.5 billion. This was more than one billion dollars higher than Mr. Wilson's first budget in 1985!

Was that progress? Here's Maz: **"Since 1984-85, we have made real progress in a changing uncertain world economy."** (*Budget*, p. 3) When facing disaster, call it progress. After breaking promises, say **"We kept our word."**

What was in store for Canadians?

Mr. Mazankowski announced that the deficit for 1993-94 would be $32.6 billion — the fourth highest in Canada's history. But even that seems optimistic. During April-May, the first two months of 1993-94, the deficit grew by $8.3 billion, almost twice as much as during the April-May in 1992.

But we're not to worry. Mazankowski adopted the Wilson remedy for failure: make rosy predictions about the distant future and blame the Liberals for present disasters.

Mazankowski devoted an entire section of his 1993 Budget to blaming the Liberals. He entitled it: **"Fiscal excesses before 1984-85 caused the deficit-debt spiral."** He then went on to predict that under his own wise guidance, the deficit would fall to $14 billion by 1996-97. Mazankowski failed to mention that Michael Wilson in 1990 had promised to reduce the deficit to $14 billion by 1993-94.

It's awesome. For these people, repeated failure breeds rising confidence. Obviously Ms. Campbell is wonderfully confident. Like Wilson 10 years ago, she too dashes off a five-year plan to eliminate the deficit. If experience means anything, Canadians know what to expect.

12.

MEANWHILE ...

WHILE WILSON AND MAZANKOWSKI WERE CHOKING the economy and piling up the government debt, the other members of the Mulroney team were busy in the same cause.

First it was the turn of the Minister of Employment and Immigration, Barbara MacDougall. In 1985, as Minister of State (Finance), she shied away from all responsibility for the collapse of the Canadian Commercial Bank and the Northland Bank, and this despite her admitted responsibility for the administration of the *Bank Act*. In 1989 she repeated that performance as the minister responsible for breaking her government's campaign promises concerning the unemployment insurance program.

During the campaign, when there were suggestions that a Conservative government would cut back the U.I. program, Trade Minister John Crosbie responded: **"It's complete nonsense."** Why, he had it straight from Mulroney himself: **"You're damn right I asked him (prime minister) about it. And he said no. No one is planning any changes in the unemployment insurance program."** (*St. John's Evening Telegram*, Oct. 14/88) If there were to be any changes, they would come only years in the future:

"We'll be looking at it (the UI program) in a couple of years, presumably to see what improvements can be made or whatever, but there are no changes planned in UI." (*Montreal Gazette*, Oct. 14/88)

The program was so healthy that one week before election day the government announced a reduction in UI premiums. Then less than five months after the election, on April 11, 1989, the government released a white paper on UI. From that document and Wilson's Budget two weeks later, flowed Bill C-21, a bill which changed U.I. profoundly.

And what about the campaign promise?

MEANWHILE...

Crosbie had left the clear impression that the government wouldn't even look at possible changes for "a couple of years." Again, what was said was not true. Minister Macdougall's testimony before a committee of the House of Commons on October 3, 1989, shows that the government was looking at changes to the UI program at the very time Crosbie was issuing his categorical denial. She said:

> **"In terms of when we began doing this, certainly it was before the election that I suggested to my officials that we should be looking at training options to get us ready for this world that we saw coming. Then we went off, like everyone else in this room, and pounded the pavement for three months."** (*Legislative Committee on Bill C-21*, Issue 19, p. 46)

So, apparently while she was pounding the pavement and while Crosbie was telling Canadians there were no such plans, her officials were following her direct orders to overhaul the program.

Bill C-21 introduced two important changes to unemployment insurance. The first change was the elimination of government contributions to the Fund.

Since its inception, the UI Program had been funded by contributions from employees, employers, and the federal government. The government's share was approximately 25% of the total cost. Bill C-21 eliminated the government's contribution. Since premiums would now have to cover the entire cost of the program, premiums were increased. Increased premiums would bring Mr. Wilson an additional $425 million in revenues in 1989-90, and an additional $1.9 billion the following year. In effect this was a very big tax increase. As we've seen, it was followed by another big premium increase - 24% - just two years later.

Except for the United States, Canada is now the only country in the industrialized western world where the government does not contribute to unemployment insurance. No longer is it a partner in the program, no matter how high unemployment climbs.

The second important change announced by the Mulroneyites was that thereafter UI funds would be used to pay for job training.

Sounds good, but its hidden vice is that the money taken away from virtually all the unemployed would be used to help train a select few, including individuals who already had jobs. For the unemployed it would become more difficult to qualify for UI, and for those who did qualify, benefits would be reduced — up to 13 fewer weeks of benefits even in regions of the country where unemployment was above 12%. For others, waiting periods would be increased.

In its first term, the Mulroney government syphoned hundreds of millions of dollars out of job training. Now it was putting some money back, but every single penny of that money was coming from the unemployed themselves.

Bill C-21 met with incredulity and hostility in every region of the country and from every labour and social group. And many employers were unhappy because they were facing higher UI premiums. But the Mulroney team, practicing what Kim Campbell calls "the politics of inclusion," refused to budge. Notwithstanding public demonstrations and a prolonged battle with the Senate, it finally forced the bill through with the help of the eight GST senators. It was passed just in time for the recession, as Canadians in the hundreds of thousands lost their jobs.

The Mulroney team took another swipe at the UI program early in 1993. Benefits were reduced from 60% to 57% of insurable earnings. For those who voluntarily left their jobs, there would be no benefits whatsoever, no matter how long they had been paying into the fund. Only if they could prove to bureaucrats that working conditions had been absolutely intolerable would they receive benefits.

Unemployed Canadians will find no friend in Prime Minister Campbell. She recently has hinted that she will bring even more sweeping changes to the UI program. (*Ottawa Citizen*, July 22/93)

Another broken promise that affects hundreds of thousands of Canadians relates to rail passenger service. During the 1988 election campaign, a letter sent from the Prime Minister's office stated:

The plan is for specific capital programs to enhance the quality and reliability of VIA's services. ... commitment is made to expand the dollar amount and improve the service of VIA Rail. (*Hansard*, June 6/89, p. 2663)

MEANWHILE...

That is what Prime Minister Mulroney's office was saying on October 14, 1988.

On August 19, 1988, just a few weeks before he called the election, Mr. Mulroney visited Acton Vale, Quebec. He crowed that he had reinstated the town's passenger rail service.

"Brian Mulroney and his team have kept their word," he boasted, speaking to a crowd of several hundred in front of the town's train station ..."We kept our word. We are people who keep our word." (*Toronto Star*, Oct. 5/89)

So what happened?

Mr. Wilson announced in his 1989 budget that funding for VIA was being cut by $500 million over five years. The other shoe dropped on October 4, 1989, when the Minister of Transport, Benoît Bouchard, announced that over half the VIA rail network was being shut down.

And what about the train to Acton Vale?

The train Mulroney and his wife proudly rode into town on that day - along with son Nicolas, who wore a *VIA Rail* cap as the television cameras whirred away - has been cancelled along with half of VIA's other services. (*Toronto Star*, Oct. 5/89)

Train service was cut across the entire country. Eighteen of VIA's 38 routes were eliminated. The number of trains running every week was slashed from 405 to 191. In the House of Commons, Mr. Mulroney declared **"I am saying we have saved VIA Rail"**. (*Hansard*, Oct. 4/89, p. 4300) His announcement of a Royal Commission on transportation would make no difference; while the Commission studied, the cuts would proceed on schedule.

One of the trains eliminated was the "Canadian", a transcontinental train which ran through southern Saskatchewan and Alberta. But saved was the northern "Super-Continental," that went through Edmonton. This decision was somewhat difficult to explain.

The northern line linking Toronto to Vancouver carried 174,000 passengers in 1988, one-third of the 539,000 pas-

sengers who took the Canadian, which originated in Montreal and went through Calgary on the way to Vancouver. As well, the SuperContinental recovered only 36 per cent of its costs from tickets, compared to 47 per cent for the Canadian. (*Edmonton Journal*, Oct. 5/89)

Canadians were asked to believe that it was only coincidence that the less profitable and less frequently used northern route ran through Deputy Prime Minister Mazankowski's riding, External Affairs Minister Clark's riding, and Defence Minister McKnight's riding.

Atlantic Canada, as usual, was hit particularly hard. In Nova Scotia, the southern service to Yarmouth was cut, as was the northern route from Truro to Sydney.

The only passenger service remaining will be a train running between Halifax and Montreal six days a week.

The slashing of service came after a year in which trains in the region were often filled to capacity and a multitude of groups pleaded with the federal government to keep them running. (*Globe and Mail*, Oct. 5/89)

A committee of the House of Commons, made up of members from all three parties, recommended that the VIA cuts be delayed until the Royal Commission had presented its report. The Mulroney government refused.

Visitors from Europe were just as perplexed as most Canadians.

"In highly industrialized countries like Canada, an efficient high-speed rail system is crucial to economic growth and progress," Dr. Wolfgang Henn, a director of the German Federal Railway, told an Ottawa seminar.

"It is the way of the future and I think it will be a mistake for Canada to cut back on its rail services. They have to modernize." (*Ottawa Citizen*, Dec. 13/89)

The assistant executive director of the French National Railway, Pierre-Louis Rochet, commented:

MEANWHILE...

"It is strange that while Europe and other industrialized countries are going in one direction, Canada is moving in the opposite direction". (Ibid.)

Back in 1981, Don Mazankowski was keenly aware of

"...the deep feeling which exists in the hearts and minds of Canadians about the fact that rail passenger service is a link which binds this country together and keeps it united. To many it is more important than the Constitution. It is a fundamental part of confederation. We would not have been a country had it not been for the guarantees inherent in the provision of rail services." (*Hansard*, Oct. 20/81, p. 11979)

As Deputy Prime Minister that same Don Mazankowski helped reduce by half that **"link which binds this country together and keeps it united."**

There were more strains on the Canadian confederation. The Prime Minister declared his counry's constitution not worth the paper it was written on and, in addition to dismantling constitutionally important social programs, pursued Free Trade with the United States and followed a policy with respect to the Post Office which further eroded the pan Canadian presence of the national government.

Since 1986 the Mulroney team has shut down or privatized more than 1400 rural post offices. The residents of many a small rural community have seen their gathering place, the building with the Canadian flag overhead, shut down. Railway lines are abandoned, post offices are boarded up. Rural Canadians now wonder about their place in this country.

The *Debates* of the House of Commons record how many MPs rose to present petitions from their constituents pleading to save their post office, but all to no avail. No matter how many signatures were presented, the result was always the same. The people were ignored and the post offices closed.

Where was Kim Campbell and her **"politics of inclusion"** when Canadians were asking to be heard? She was there, but she refused to listen.

And she was there, refusing to heed the outcry against the legislation to appease, once again, international pharmaceutical corporations in their relentless attack on Canada's successful program to keep drug prices under control. What was it these companies were so determined to destroy? We have to go back to 1923.

Since 1923 the *Patent Act* had provided that an international patent on a pharmaceutical would not apply if the active ingredient was <u>manufactured</u> in Canada. For almost 70 years, therefore, we have recognized that patents granted for life-saving medicines were not to be treated in the same fashion as patents widgets or mousetraps.

In 1923 there was hope that compulsory licences to manufacture fine chemicals would bring some competition to the marketplace for pharmaceuticals. Unfortunately, Canada's economy was too small to support the investment required to manufacture fine chemicals; consequently, the provision had virtually no impact. The anticipated competition failed to materialize and drug prices went higher and higher.

By the early 1960s, drug prices had become an explosive public issue. The government at that time responded slowly, buying time by holding a series of public inquiries, including a Royal Commission. They all came to the conclusion that Canadian drug prices were among the highest in the world.

The drug makers disagreed. In 1966, Dr. Wiggle of the Pharmaceutical Manufacturers Association of Canada (PMAC) argued before a Special House of Commons Committee that

> **"Our deliberations...impelled us to the fundamental conclusion that the cost of drugs to Canadians is fair and reasonable."** (***Special Committee on Drug Costs and Prices***, **June 16/66, p. 94**)

He then recommended **"...a wider availability of drug insurance to prevent catastrophic drug expenses during medical emergencies."** (Ibid. p. 96)

So, Dr. Wiggle and PMAC believed that although drug prices could lead to catastrophic drug expenses, those prices were reasonable.

MEANWHILE...

The remedy was insurance. But Canadians were angry. In 1969, a majority Liberal government responded by introducing compulsory licensing for the *importation* of fine chemicals. This meant that a company could import drugs from outside the country, package them here in Canada, and sell them on the market under the supervision of the Ministry of Health and Welfare in return for paying a royalty to the patent holder. This measure to encourage competition, which saved Canadians hundreds of millions of dollars, infuriated the multinational drug companies, although between 1967 and 1982, the average profits for the drug industry were still among the highest of all Canadian industries. Profit levels for the Canadian pharmaceutical industry exceeded those of all manufacturing industries and appeared to be higher than those in Japan, Germany, France, and Switzerland. However, they were not as high as profit levels in the United States.

To make matters worse, some influential people in the United States were publically admiring Canada's effective system on drug prices. If Canada's system spread to the U.S., — the really important market — the drug companies' profits there might also be reduced. Something had to be done to stamp out the Canadian system.

So the companies lobbied the government relentlessly to rescind compulsory licensing. Finally, with the election of Brian Mulroney, they found a sympathetic ear. It was sympathetic in part because they had got their message to the President of the United States.

After President Reagan and Prime Minister Mulroney met at the Shamrock Summit in Quebec City on March 18, 1985, they released a joint declaration. That declaration in part stated:

> **"We have also *directed* that action be undertaken over the next twelve months to resolve specific impediments to trade... Such action...will concentrate initially on...cooperation to protect *intellectual property rights* from trade in counterfeit goods and other abuses of copyright and patent law."**

No one has alleged that Canada had difficulties with provisions in U.S. copyright and patent law. However, the United States government had bought the drug companies' argument and so considered the compulsory licensing provisions of our patent law as an "irritant." The reference in the Shamrock Summit declaration was aimed at *our* patent laws, not at the laws of the United States. In the declaration, Canada's prime minister, in effect, condemned his own country as an abuser of patent law.

When Prime Minister Mulroney met with President Reagan in Washington the following year, in March of 1986, a senior administration official was asked what trade issues had been discussed. He replied: **"We had Gulf and Western, we had lumber, pharmaceuticals. Those were the three."** (*Toronto Star*, Dec. 7/86)

On April 7, 1986, U.S. trade representative Clayton Yeutter said that the Canadian government had repeatedly promised to revise its patent legislation for pharmaceuticals, but that nothing had happened. **"We've been exercising uncommon patience, but even our patience wears thin."** (*Ottawa Citizen*, June 28/86)

In the summer of 1986, then Vice-President George Bush came to Canada. He told reporters **"that he raised the 'problems with pharmaceuticals' during meetings with Canadian officials, adding that, 'there are many people in the United States that feel very strongly about it. I made that point, but I would like to see the matter resolved... '."** (*Toronto Sun*, June 19/86)

Following the visit by Vice-President Bush, the government, on June 27, on the very last day before the summer recess, unsuccessfully attempted to introduce their new drug bill. Unable to introduce it in the House of Commons, the government instead released it to the public as a government document. The document was carefully examined south of the border.

The Office of the United States Trade Representative, in its 1986 Report on "Foreign Trade Barriers" dealt at length with specific Canadian trade irritants. One of the irritants was **"compulsory pharmaceutical patents licensing."** The report states that compulsory licensing, which was introduced in 1969, **"was designed to rectify perceived problems and foster greater pharmaceutical industry competition. The law is highly popular."** The report went on to state:

MEANWHILE...

Canada announced the terms of legislation it will introduce in the late fall of 1986 to modify Canada's patent law. This proposed bill is being reviewed to see whether it would provide acceptable patent protection standards.

The Americans reviewed Canada's draft bill. Apparently they came to the conclusion that it was not completely acceptable to them, because when the bill was introduced in November, 1986, the powers of the prices review board had been reduced, and the availability of compulsory licences was restricted even further.

The report of the United States Trade Representative also noted that the Canadian law **"cost U.S. pharmaceutical interests significant lost revenue each year."** Obviously if the U.S. administration got the legislation it wanted, U.S. pharmaceutical interests stood to gain "significant" revenues each year, revenues collected from Canadians.

When the Mulroneyites introduced Bill C-22, the drug patent legislation, they insisted that it was for the benefit of Canadians and was completely unrelated to the trade negotiations then taking place.

When the Minister of Consumer and Corporate Affairs, Harvie Andre, appeared before the Senate Special Committee on Bill C-22 on July 7, 1987, he stated categorically that the bill **"has nothing to do with free trade."** Again, he said, **"Bill C-22 is not part of the free trade discussions."** (Issue 19, p. 24) He told the Committee: **"I have asked Mr. Reisman whether this subject has ever come up at any of his negotiations at any time or any place, and he has said 'no'."**

The text of the FTA was agreed to by the negotiators on October 3/88. The text, dated October 3, was released by the Canadian embassy in Whashington shortly after the deal had been struck. But it was quickly recalled by officials. They claimed that typographical errors had to be corrected. A new version, dated October 4, was distributed. Unfortunately for the government, the original version found its way to the *Globe and Mail* which revealed that it contained the following provision, which did not appear in the October 4 version:

Canada has agreed to pass the pending amendments contained in Bill C-22 in respect of compulsory licensing of pharmaceuticals. (*Globe and Mail*, Oct. 9/87)

THE SHOW MUST NOT GO ON

The page on which this clause appeared was initialled by Germain Denis, one of Canada's trade negotiators. When this document was made public by the *Globe and Mail*, the Mulroneyites had some trouble explaining why something that had absolutely nothing to do with free trade, something that had not even been raised in the discussions, was dealt with explicitly in the text approved by one of our negotiators.

When a question about the October 3 text was asked in the House of Commons, the Deputy Prime Minister, Mr. Mazankowski, said:

> "I do not know of such a document..." (*Hansard*, Oct. 9/87, p. 9865)

He continued:

> "Just because the Hon. Member (Brian Tobin) does not like the honest answers that are given, it should not give him a licence to suggest that everything that comes from this side of the House is dishonest."

Mr. Andre, the Minister of Health and Welfare, resorted to a simple stonewall, insisting:

> "Bill C-22 was not part of the trade negotiations." (*Hansard*, Oct. 9/87, p. 9869)

Mr. Andre was contradicted by the Honourable Pat Carney, then Minister for International Trade who that very same day released a written statement:

> "One such working party sent forward to the negotiators a draft initialled by the working party chiefs recommending the commitment by the Government of Canada with respect to C-22."

> The Canadian negotiating team rejected this proposal that was brought forward by a working party in the final stages of the negotiations. This was part of the natural process of these negotiations. (*Globe and Mail*, Oct. 10/87)

MEANWHILE...

In the Senate, Government Leader Lowell Murray had yet another perspective.

> "If the Senate were to defeat Bill C-22, I believe that many congressmen and senators in the United States would think twice about their support for the Free Trade Agreement, because, surely, they would take such action as meaning that one of the houses of the Canadian Parliament was thumbing its nose at the spirit of this free trade agreement."(*Debates*, Oct. 9/87, p. 1923)

He was subsequently contradicted by Michael Wilson, who said:

> "...if Bill C-22 does not go ahead, one thing will be very clear, it will not affect the free trade agreement." (*Hansard*, Oct. 19/87, p. 10132)

What was the view in the United States of the relationship between Bill C-22 and the FTA? The *Washington Post* of October 17, 1987, carried a story headlined, "**U.S. Bowed to Canadian Demands to Change Pact.**"

> Reagan administration sources who were close to the final negotiations said the drug issue was part of the deal when Wilson stepped to the window of the Treasury Building just before midnight Saturday and gave a thumbs-up sign to signal there was an agreement.
>
> By Sunday morning, however, the Canadians had a change of heart the U.S. sources said, and insisted that the drug section had to be dropped from the agreement.
>
> That demand was a subject of tense talks throughout the day, interrupted late Sunday afternoon for a joint U.S.-Canadian press conference hailing the agreement. No mention was made at that press conference of the continuing dispute over the drug issue, which was not resolved until 10:30 Sunday night when the United States gave in.
>
> They gave in to not mentioning the drug patent legislation in the Agreement, but only because to mention it would show Canadians

had been mislead by the Canadian government. The *Washington Post* article continues:

> **But a U.S. summary of the agreement, released at 6:30 Sunday evening, said the accord contained a clause "to make progress toward establishing adequate and effective protection of pharmaceuticals in Canada by liberalizing compulsory licensing provisions."**
>
> **And a midafternoon draft of a briefing paper for Yeutter and Baker referred to the provisions on changing the drug patent law, calling it "one of the principal and longest standing trade irritants in our bilateral relations."**

This contradicts everything Canadians were told. In support of the *Washington Post* story, remember the October 3rd version of the agreement had, in fact, been signed by Michael Wilson, Pat Carney, Derek Burney and Simon Reisman. Mr. Wilson was asked about that.

> *Mr. LaPierre:* **Mr. Speaker, is the Minister of Finance telling me that the Canadian Ambassador in Washington distributed a forged document to reporters the first time around?**
>
> *Mr. Wilson:* **(Etobicoke Centre): Yes, Mr. Speaker, that is a false document. That document was not signed, it was not part of the agreement.** (*Hansard*, Oct. 15/87, p. 9999)

But it was signed. It was signed by Mr. Wilson himself! Bill C-22 was a cave-in to foreign interests. It was a made-in-America policy for the benefit of American pharmaceutical companies and was against the interest of Canadian consumers.

Notwithstanding all the evidence, Mr. Andre follows the established policy — admit nothing. He continued to claim:

> "**Bill C-22 is a made-in-Canada policy for Canadians. It is in no way tied to pressure from American multinational drug companies or to free-trade negotiations with the U.S."** (*Edmonton Journal*, Nov. 6/87)

It is an old technique. You simply deny the facts, and hope that by the time an election rolls around the people will have forgotten.

Bill C-22 provided that brand name companies would have a ten-year period of market exclusivity, or monopoly, for their

MEANWHILE...

products — seven years if their generic competitor manufactured the active ingredient in Canada. Clearly, the brand name multinational pharmaceutical manufacturers were the primary beneficiaries of this scheme. The opportunity for Canadian generic companies to market copies of brand name drugs was severely curtailed. Free from generic competition, the brand name companies were able to utilize their monopoly position to charge a far higher price for their products than they had been able to do previously.

Why else would the brand name companies have lobbied so strenuously and expensively in support of the bill? Surely it was not because they wanted to benefit Canadians with lower prices. They could have done that without Parliament's permission. Surely it was not because their parent companies in the United States, Britain and Switzerland wanted to transfer their research laboratories to Canada. That could have been done without the blessing of Canada's Parliament.

Corporations the world over are in business to make money, not for some altruistic purpose. In its simplest terms, brand name companies demanded the bill because it afforded them the opportunity to maximize profits in a monopoly environment. Foreign governments supported this bill because increased profits made in Canada would flow to companies based in their territories. Conversely, generic firms were opposed to the bill because it limited their profits by restricting their ability to market new drugs. Consumers were also opposed to the legislation because they feared higher prices for prescription medicines.

When the smoke cleared in November of 1987, it was the foreign interests that had prevailed, not the Canadian interests. Bill C-22 had passed.

But that is not the end of the story. The PMAC and Washington came back demanding more.

Though the pharmaceutical companies had achieved a great deal with Bill C-22, they had not succeeded in their primary objective, which was the total elimination of compulsory licensing.

In 1987, while the Bill C-22 battle was raging, PMAC and its member companies had nothing but praise for the legislation.

Stuart Alexander, the President of the Upjohn Company of Canada, told the Special Senate Committee:

"The passage of Bill C-22 will provide a healthy environment for both the innovative and the generic industries." (June 11/87, Issue 15, p. 50)

Pierre Fortin, of PMAC, told the Senate Committee on Banking, Trade and Commerce:

"Bill C-22, as passed by the House of Commons, is a fair and balanced compromise which will benefit all Canadians." (Oct. 1/87, Issue 36, p. 93)

Judy Erola, of PMAC, told the same committee:

"...Bill C-22 is a compromise, full of checks and balances, that is good public policy for Canada." (Oct. 1/87, Issue 36, p. 80)

The following month she declared that the passage of Bill C-22 **"means the beginning of a new era in Canadian biomedical research."** (*PMAC Press Release,* Nov. 19/87)

One year later, immediately following the 1988 election, the **"new era"** was over. The **"fair and balanced compromise"** was no longer fair enough and not balanced correctly. Canada was still an outlaw regime which was persecuting the international drug companies. Washington and the American drug companies demanded more concessions; the Mulroney team obliged again.

On June 23, 1992, the Mulroney government introduced Bill C-91 and rammed it through Parliament, brushing off all opposition. The legislation increased patents to 20 years and abolished compulsory licensing. Why was this being done? Michael Wilson had the answer:

"We are doing this at this time because it is in our best interest. It is good for Canada, and it is good for Canadians". (*Senate Standing Committee on Banking, Trade and Commerce,* Issue 28, p. 124)

And the American drug companies that wanted it, companies like Eli Lilly and Co., agreed. Its President, Mr. Vaugh Bryson, said in his company's 1991 Annual Report:

"The tentacles of governmental planning are slowly gripping the health care systems of many western nations."

Of course for his company's sake, Mr. Bryson wants as little government interference as possible in any health care system — that system is his market.

Michael Wilson told the Senate Committee:

"This bill is about seniors. This bill is about children."(p. 124)

Children? In the United States, 40% to 60% of children do not get vaccinated. In inner city neighbourhoods, up to 90% do not get vaccinated! When the Clinton administration, as part of their health care system, proposed to distribute vaccines free of charge to doctors' offices throughout the country, the pharmaceutical companies were outraged, even though they would be paid for the vaccines by the government. It would be interference in their market and with the prices and profits they want to control.

According to the *New York Times* of February 1, 1993, **"the full battery of recommended vaccines, when bought by private doctors in the open market, rose to $244 in 1992, from $23 in 1982."**

Now the U.S. government was to buy in bulk and distribute free. The companies' retail market would disappear. No longer would they be able to increase their price by 200, or 300, or 400% on vaccines designed to prevent diseases such as rubella and polio.

And the millions of children who don't get vaccinated because the price of the vaccine is too high for their parents to afford? The companies are getting more than enough money from those families who can pay. While up to 90% of children in inner city neighbourhoods do not get vaccinated, government "tentacles" must be kept out of health care.

Those are the companies that, through their Canadian subsidiaries and the PMAC, came to Canada and said that we should adopt their drug patent system because it would be good for us and good for *our* health care system.

That's how, as Minister for International Trade, Michael Wilson sacrificed an important part of our health care system to foreign interests. Now, as he goes into retirement, he urges Canadians to support Kim Campbell. He is confident that she will carry on his policies.

13.

"A NEW STANDARD OF MORALITY"

THE *TORONTO STAR* OF JULY 24, 1993, alleged that **"Prime Minister Kim Campbell has inherited the mandate of one of the most corrupt governments in Canadian history."** Is this true? Was Richard Cleroux right when he said that Canadians **"have lived through the most corruption-ridden federal government in our history"**? Earlier, we saw evidence that he may have been right. The *Toronto Star* has repeated and updated the charge. Let's try to finish that story.

We've seen how, on May 15, 1986, just hours after Prime Minister Brian Mulroney proclaimed his new standard for political morality, Conservative MP Michele Gravel was charged with 50 counts of political corruption by the RCMP. For two-and-a-half years, Mr. Gravel professed innocence and took various legal steps, including an application to the Supreme Court of Canada, to have the charges quashed. And as he was entitled to, he continued to draw his MP's salary during this period. But on December 7, 1988 immediately after the election, he pleaded guilty to 15 counts of bribery; was fined $50,000 (which was $25,000 less than he admitted receiving in bribes) and was sentenced to one year in jail.

According to the evidence, Mr. Gravel had been accepting bribes from contractors seeking government contracts. The Crown alleged he had even been accepting them within the House of Commons itself.

> [Crown prosecutor Valmont] Beaulieu said that on two occasions, cash payments were made by contractors who visited Gravel at the House of Commons.
>
> "The accused was in session," said Beaulieu, "so a House of Commons page went to fetch him. Envelopes containing money were then handed to him next to the curtains behind the members' chairs." (*Montreal Gazette*, Feb. 7/89)

A NEW STANDARD OF MORALITY

Mr. Gravel was released after serving less than two months of his sentence. The fine was paid, though not by Mr. Gravel. **"To this day Mr. Gravel says he does not know who paid his fine."** (*Globe and Mail*, Feb. 5/92) Although he had pleaded guilty, later in the year he claimed he was innocent.

> **"Asked why he pleaded guilty to the charges if he was innocent, Gravel became furious and shouted: "I don't know why, I was told it would not change anything if I pleaded not guilty... I've paid a lot for having had a party at my house.**
>
> **"I've been harassed a hell of a lot for only $40,000. A lot of other people are taking in $300,000 and $400,000... I'm so f—-ing mad. I want to kill my lawyer."**(*Montreal Gazette*, Nov. 10/89)

Apparently he believed himself innocent because he saw himself as a mere intermediary between those seeking government contracts and the Minister of Public Works, Roch LaSalle. When Revenue Canada demanded that Gravel pay tax on the bribe money he acknowledged receiving, Gravel claimed he had collected the money on LaSalle's behalf and had in fact turned it over to LaSalle. His position was that if Revenue Canada wanted to collect tax, it should look to Mr. LaSalle for satisfaction. **"I went to jail for Roche LaSalle and I'm not going to pay his income tax."** (*Globe and Mail*, Sept. 23/91) Mr. LaSalle denied the charge.

Edouard Desrosiers, another member of the Mulroney team, found himself before a criminal court judge. Shortly before the election, there were reports that the Conservative MP put in his own pocket money raised for his riding association. Deputy Prime Minister Don Mazankowski described the story as just the latest in **"rumour after rumour, innuendo after innuendo, all of which have been unfounded."** (*Globe and Mail*, Aug. 25/88) Mr. Desrosiers denied the accusations absolutely: **"I never, never received one cent."** (*Toronto Star*, Aug. 25/88). He, however, chose not to seek re-election. After the election, in February 1989, Mr. Desrosiers, was arraigned in Court on charges of fraud, breach of trust and uttering forged documents. Charges of corruption and theft were later added to the list.

On June 19, 1990, he pleaded guilty to fraud, was fined $3,000 and put on probation for a year. This conviction was now added to one he had received years earlier for his part in an armed bank robbery.

The period immediately following the 1988 election was a very busy time for members of the Mulroney team. On November 22, 1988, the day immediately following election day, the RCMP searched the offices of newly re-elected Conservative MP Richard Grisé, former chairman of Quebec Conservative caucus. They had been investigating the MP for some time and were in a position to execute a search warrant on November 14, but RCMP Chief Superintendent Brian McConnell decided to delay until after the election. He said that **"...proceeding with those searches in less than one week before a federal election... perhaps could have influenced the election on a local and national level"**. (*Montreal Gazette*, Nov. 22/89) Six days before he came to that conclusion, Peter White, Mulroney's principal secretary, had written to the RCMP about Mr. Grise. When Opposition Leader John Turner asked for information on the contents of that letter, Deputy Prime Minister Don Mazankowski refused to give it and accused Turner of **"trying to incriminate the RCMP and undermine the integrity of the RCMP."** (*Hansard*, Nov. 22/89, p. 5988)

Mr. Grisé was re-elected on November 21, 1988, his offices were searched on November 22, 1988, and on April 14, 1989, he was charged with eight counts of breach of trust and three counts of fraud. It was alleged that he had been accepting bribes and kickbacks in return for contracts. A month later, on May 23, he pleaded guilty to all charges, was fined $20,000 and sentenced to one day in jail plus three years probation. His guilty plea, like that of Mr. Gravel's, abbreviated the amount of detail in court testimony necessary for the conviction.

Though he had been convicted of fraud and breach of trust, some of Grisé's fellow Conservatives did not want him to resign as MP.

Beauce MP Gilles Bernier called Grisé's fraud and breach-of-trust activities "anomalies" and said they in no way "detract from his qualities as an MP."

Bernier praised Grisé's "dedication as an MP, as a Conservative and to his people in the riding of Chambly."(*Montreal Gazette*, May 24/89)

Montreal-Duvernay MP Vincent Della Noce, parliamentary secretary to the Revenue Minister, warned that if Mr. Grise is forced out then other people will not want to sit in the Commons. "I don't think anybody will want to come here any more."

Mr. Della Noce complained that the courts are imposing a double standard that's tougher for elected officials than for the general public. "It's becoming very nerve-wracking. We're all human. All sorts of things can happen when you're an MP."(*Globe and Mail*, May 25/89)

All sorts of things did keep happening and they kept happening even after Grisé resigned his seat on May 30/89.

Late in June, 1989, it was learned that two more Conservative MPs were under investigation by the RCMP. Prime Minister Mulroney said that such investigations were just a fact of life and that the integrity of his government was of the highest order:

"I suspect that one of the reasons that we were re-elected is that the people of Canada were expressing confidence in the Government in respect of the integrity of all of its members."(*Hansard*, June 27/89, p. 3684)

The *Montreal Gazette* of the next day reported that **"Mulroney's response startled the opposition."** It probably startled the entire country.

Conservative MP, Gilles Bernier, was next. In June 1990 he was charged with fraud and breach of trust. The charges were dismissed in October 1991, following errors allegedly made by a judge during the preliminary inquiry. The Ontario Court of Appeal disagreed with the decision and in September of 1992 ordered the criminal charges restored. More than three years after being originally charged, the member for Beauce still awaits trial.

In February 1991, Gabriel Fontaine, the former deputy whip of the Conservative Party, was charged with 14 counts of fraud, breach of trust and conspiracy. Mr. Fontaine has maintained his innocence during these past two-and-a-half years as he battles to have the charges quashed.

On August 22, 1991, Conservative MP Maurice Tremblay was charged by the RCMP with defrauding the House of Commons. On December 10, 1992, a jury convicted him following a two-week trial. He was fined $12,000. The Crown filed a notice of appeal, claiming that the fine was **"insufficient to reflect the gravity"** of the offence. (*Toronto Star*, Feb. 26/93) Mr. Tremblay, in turn, appealed the conviction, and in the meantime continues to sit in the House of Commons as the member for Lotbinière.

The most recent episode was reported by the *Montreal Gazette* on July 13, 1993.

> **Charges of influence-peddling and breach of trust were laid yesterday against Conservative MP Carole Jacques and her political organizer, Jean-Yves Pantaloni.**
>
> **The charges arise from a loan made by the federal Department of Industry, Science and Technology and a request for funds from two crown corporations.**

As we approach the 1993 election three Conservative members of the House of Commons await trial on political corruption charges. Four other members of the team have been convicted. One of those four has retained his seat in the House of Commons. All those awaiting trial said that they want to be part of the Campbell team when the election was called, though some recently have expressed second thoughts.

Is all this activity in the courts unusual?

Yes, it is.

Since the turn of the century, only three other members of the House of Commons have been convicted of political corruption.

And in addition to Conservative MPs, there were Tory organizers, officials and other functionaries. Most recently, it was the

Conservative vice-president of the Lotbinière riding association who on March 26, 1993, was convicted of fraud and fined $3,000. He had taken a vacation in Mexico with House of Commons funds.

So, has Kim Campbell inherited "one of the most corrupt governments in Canadian history"? No. Not one of the most. It has been the most corrupt. And she did not inherit this corrupt government. She was a member of it — a leading member — and was chosen to lead it at the urging and recommendation of Mulroney himself.

Though political corruption played a leading role, there are other features of this administration's record we should not forget. Let's look at a few highlights, in chronological order.

On November 21, 1989, the *Globe and Mail* reported:

Donors who contribute more than $5,000 a year to the Conservative party should be treated as a special "elite," given insider information, and invited to dine with the Prime Minister and to intimate dinners with senior cabinet ministers, according to a 1986 internal party memo about fund raising. ...

"Each regional chairman will be responsible for organizing an annual regional finance dinner to which 'blue-chip' donors will be invited for an intimate dinner with a senior cabinet minister," the report advises.

These ministers' parties, the paper states later on, would be "to provide access for donors to cabinet."

Donors were divided into tiers according to how much they donated. The report recommended that less attention be paid to the so-called **"lower-yield donors. ... This is not only cost-effective but also creates a subtle hierarchy that can motivate those at one level to attempt to move up, and reward those who contribute most."**

The chairman of the corporate strategy committee was Peter Clark, the Calgary lawyer to whom we were introduced in an earlier chapter.

When this story broke, the Tories acknowledged the authenticity of the memorandum, but denied it had ever been implemented. But they were soon caught onto again when a week later it was revealed that:

> Internal Conservative Party documents reveal a proposal that, in certain circumstances, Tory fundraisers would remind potential corporate donors of federal government contracts they have received....there were detailed plans within the Progressive Conservative Canada Fund to set up a computerized system in which the file on each corporate donor would include a list of the number of government contracts, grants or policies that have benefited that corporation.
>
> ...According to the documents, each corporate donor profile contains information on the company including the company's sales, profits, ownership, financial year-end, and "account number" with the PC Canada Fund. The profile also identifies the party's fundraiser who will make the approach and his "contact" at the company. It shows the PC fund's "target" donation, the company's "Government Relations" and whether the company will agree to be invoiced in the future for specified amounts. (*Globe and Mail*, Nov. 29/89)

Predictably, there were denials of any improprieties. Deputy Prime Minister Don Mazankowski tried his usual brush-off by saying it was **"really old news that is being rehashed,"** and that the memorandum **"has never been adopted."** (*Hansard*, Nov. 29/89, pp. 6373-4)

In November 1989, Canadians learned that while Michael Wilson was preaching restraint and cutting their social programs, hundreds of thousands of dollars were being lent by the Federal Business Development Bank to help finance Ottawa-area strip clubs. Industry Minister Harvie Andre said the Bank's lending rules were being revised, but offered no other explanation.

In September 1988, after George Hees left the cabinet, he was named Mulroney's personal representative and ambassador-at-large, with a mandate to keep his eye on Canada's food aid programs. He reported directly to the Prime Minister.

> Hees gets a salary of between $101,400 and $132,400 annually. He also gets a parliamentary pension of about $90,000.
>
> The former minister has a staff of four - a chauffeur, "special adviser," executive assistant and secretary - as well as a government car and a liberal travel budget.
>
> In 1989-90, Hees was given a budget of $612,000; $300,000 for salaries and $312,000 for operating expenses, which includes travel. The money is allocated through External Affairs. (*Ottawa Citizen*, April 5/90)

Canadians seem to find that a bit hard to swallow when, as we have already seen, Mr. Wilson, in his 1989 budget, cut millions of dollars in food aid for the impoverished.

January of 1990, like many previous Januaries, was a trying time for the Conservatives. This time it was Sports Minister Jean Charest who was making headlines.

> Quebec Superior Court Judge Yvan Macerola said in Montreal he had received a call from Charest about a case before him but had refused to talk to him. (*Ottawa Citizen*, Jan. 24/90)

Though his version of events was a little different, Charest denied that he had acted improperly.

> "There was absolutely no interference in the case, not before, not during," he said.
>
> "But one of the parties requested that I call the judge. And when I phoned and I spoke to the judge, it was quite clear that he did not wish that and that's where the matter stood."
>
> He said the call for his resignation "is obviously based on not knowing at all what's going on here... What else do you expect from the opposition?" (*Ibid.*)

The following day, he faxed his letter of resignation to Mulroney from Aukland, New Zealand. Later Charest was rehabilitated. Now he is the Deputy Prime Minister of Canada.

Several days later, there was another resignation. This time it was Brian Gallery, who stepped down as vice chairman of Canadian National Railways. He had been a Board member since 1986 and acting chairman from 1987 to 1989.

> **Mr. Gallery, [was] a close friend of Prime Minister Brian Mulroney, and the chairman of the Progressive Conservatives' elite fundraising wing, the 500 Club....(*Globe and Mail*, Feb. 2/90)**

The *Globe and Mail* was not exaggerating in calling him a "close" friend of Mr. Mulroney's.

> **In an interview with *The Globe* in 1987, Mr. Gallery admitted that he had used the chairman's railway car to take a group of eight Montreal friends to Mr. Mulroney's birthday party at 24 Sussex Dr. in Ottawa. (*Globe and Mail*, Feb. 2/90)**

Mr. Gallery's real difficulties arose out of a letter he wrote to CN on July 7, 1989, complaining about CN's decision to cut its advertising in a magazine he owned. He feared that if other companies followed suit, it **"would be a serious blow to the financial success of Gallery Publications."** He suggested that CN's plan to cut advertising costs could be accomplished **"by cancelling advertisements in other publications or newspapers...."** (copy of letter)

Mr. Gallery addressed this letter to Mr. Ducey, Vice-President in charge of Public Affairs and Advertising, and he wrote it while acting chairman of CN.

When the letter became public, the chairman of CN, Brian Smith, launched an investigation. On February 8, 1990, he concluded:

> **I consider that Mr. Gallery was wrong to place himself in apparent and direct conflict between his interest as a publisher and his duty as a Director and acting Chairman of CN. In so doing, he breached the fundamental principles of the Conflict Code.... (Report to the Minister of Transport)**

A NEW STANDARD OF MORALITY

These events were thought to have had some effect on the polls which reflected the growing unpopularity of the Conservative government. Mr. Mulroney did not seem to think so.

> "We're not particularly popular anywhere right now.... That's what happens to a government when you try to do some pretty tough things - you lose popularity. We're not here to win a popularity contest; we're here to run the country." (*Globe and Mail*, Feb. 15/90)

Exactly, but it was precisely the way he was running the country that dismayed Canadians.

Just a few days after he mused publically about the reasons for his unpopularity, details of his 1989 trip to the Far East and Costa Rica were made public. By the time all the bills came in, the 19-day trip would cost taxpayers approximately $750,000.

> "It may look expensive but we travel cheap, with the minimum support staff" necessary to operate the Prime Minister's Office abroad, said Mr. Mulroney's spokesman, Gilbert Lavoie. "Other countries' leaders travel much more expensively." (*Globe and Mail*, Feb. 21/90)

Wrong. As part of this trip, Mr. Mulroney attended the Commonwealth Conference in Malaysia. The same newspaper article reported that the Canadian delegation, which included 32 aides and technicians, was the largest among the 49 member countries at the conference.

The style at the Francophone Summit in 1989 was not very different. The *Toronto Star* of March 19, 1990, reported that flying Mila Mulroney home from the May 1989 Francophone Summit had cost $104,000.

The recession didn't seem to figure. The PC Leader had this to say on July 30/90:

> "I don't believe the economy is in recession, or approaching a point of recession....The economy is doing what Mr. Wilson thought the economy must do...." (*Globe and Mail*)

When he spoke those words, the country was already in recession. Statistics Canada figures show that the recession began in the

THE SHOW MUST NOT GO ON

second quarter of 1990, months before those soothing words were uttered. Meanwhile, stories that caused Canadians to shake their heads continued to unfold.

In June 1990, Canadians learned the facts surrounding the 1986 privatization of CN's trucking division, CN Route. It had revenues of $150 million, 3,400 employees and 53 terminals across the country. Mulroney and his cabinet colleagues agreed to sell the **"$100-million Crown-owned trucking company to a buyer for $29 million despite a 1986 check showing he had so many financial troubles he couldn't even get a credit card."** (*Ottawa Citizen*, June 4/90)

Mr. Manfred Ruhland, who had declared bankruptcy in 1981, got together with some associates and persuaded the Conservatives to sell them the company using the crown corporation's own money. In a leveraged buyout, they took mortgages on prime real estate owned by CN Route and used those funds to pay for the company. As the Ottawa Citizen put it, they bought the company **"without paying a nickel of their own money."**

A week after "buying" the company, Mr. Ruhland went on a **"spending frenzy."** He took his wife, children and mother on a $17,000 holiday to Austria, with the bill going to the company.

> ...Ruhland got back from his Austrian holiday just in time to take delivery of a boat he ordered, a 390 Sea Ray, for $125,000. He called it Route I.
>
> ...A year later, Ruhland sold that boat and bought another, a $690,000 Sea Ray 460 that he called Route II.
>
> ...The burly, one-time constable with the Ontario Provincial Police paid himself a salary of $175,000 a year, plus travel and entertainment expenses. For his top executives, Route Canada leased Jaguars or Cadillacs, complete with cellular phones and fax machines.
>
> ...The day Ruhland closed the deal with the government, he incorporated a company named Manair Leasing Ltd. A few months later, Manair paid about $3.5 million for a Beechcraft 300 turbo prop. Ruhland financed the purchase of the plane with a loan from Royal Bank, and took possession

A NEW STANDARD OF MORALITY

in mid-1987. But Route Canada cash actually paid for the plane. (*Toronto Star*, June 6/90)

The airplane was used for frequent trips to West Palm Beach and Nassau, for "bank meetings." In less than two years the company was bankrupt. Canada's second largest trucking firm was finished. All the employees lost their jobs and creditors were left owed $60 million. Among the bills that had not been paid were employee income tax deductions to Revenue Canada, union dues, pension contributions, workers compensation payments and health care premiums.

Even the money deducted from salaries to make court-ordered support payments was held back, not turned over to divorced mothers who relied on the funds to pay the bills. (*Toronto Star*, June 10/90)

While $21 million owed to government and employee benefit plans went unpaid, other bills were taken care of, including:

$685,000 to Camp Associates, an advertising firm that did a glossy launch campaign for Route Canada that included ads in newspapers and magazines, a December, 1986, kick-off party at the Metro Convention Centre and a variety of promotional items, including golf tees and miniature trucks.

Hugh Segal, the president of the holding company that owns Camp Associates, said his firm signed an ad contract with Ruhland and the Fingolds in August, 1986. That was four months before Ruhland and his partners took control of Route Canada. (*Toronto Star*, June 10/90)

Hugh Segal later became the Prime Minister's Chief of Staff.

Any admission of wrongdoing or even error? No. The Mulroney team pleaded innocence: all they had done was to privatize the company.

What about Mr. Ruhland? — the Mulroney team's choice to take over CN Route? **"I haven't done anything wrong, so why should I be worried?"** (*Toronto Star*, June 10/90)

Canadians were also expected to believe that there was nothing wrong when the government announced that small regional immigration offices across the country would close and be replaced by a national mail-in immigration-processing centre located in Vegreville, Alberta. Though Canadians thought this was a joke, the Mulroney team was serious. Vegreville is in Deputy Prime Minister Don Mazankowski's riding.

Tory lobbyists were, of course, very active throughout this period. Interesting stories about their activities arose on a regular basis, but one of the most interesting involve Telesat, the government owned communications company. When the CRTC limited its rate increase to 2.7%, the company appealed the decision to cabinet. To help them with the appeal, Telesat hired four lobbyists. They were:

> **Bill Fox, Prime Minister Brian Mulroney's former press secretary; William Jarvis, former Conservative Party president; Elizabeth Roscoe, who served as an assistant to Barbara McDougall....and Harry Near, who at one time worked for former Tory cabinet minister and now Senator Patricia Carney. (*Globe and Mail*, Apr. 12/91)**

It was a remarkable situation. Liberal MP and communications critic, Sheila Finestone put it best:

> **"You've got the government which owns the company Telesat essentially, paying top Conservative lobbyists to lobby their own Conservative government. I think that's pretty sleazy." (Ibid.)**

When Tories were not being paid to lobby the Mulroney government, they got jobs with companies awarded contracts by the Mulroney government.

> **A lucrative contract to study how Canada should deliver foreign aid to the Third World was awarded last year to a company founded by a key adviser to Prime Minister Brian Mulroney.**

> **Just two months after the $700,000 "strategic management review" of the Canadian International Development Agency (CIDA) was given to Secor Inc. of Montreal, company founder Marcel Cote quit the Prime Minister's Office and rejoined the firm.**

A NEW STANDARD OF MORALITY

In an interview yesterday, Cote said he owned no shares in Secor during the 16 months he was Mulroney's director of strategic planning....

Cote who re-purchased his interest in Secor when he left, said his conduct does not contravene the conflict-of-interest rules for ex-government appointees. (*Toronto Star*, May 24/91)

As Canadians watched this largess for the few, they were again told to expect less for themselves. As Tories prepared for their party's general meeting in Toronto, they openly discussed further cuts to social programs, including health care.

"Whittling back the costs of medicare and other social programs are at the very top of the Conservative agenda," says Don Blenkarn (Mississauga South). (*Toronto Star*, Aug. 6/91)

Not much concern was expressed about the 120,000 men, women and children in Toronto on welfare — an increase of 85% in the past year. Following the convention, a poll was released showing only 12% of Canadians approved of the Mulroney government's performance — he had fallen to pre-teen levels, the lowest in polling history.

1992 followed the pattern firmly established over the previous years. Though his popularity lagged as badly as the economy, Mulroney began the new year saying: **"My expectation is to lead the party into the next election and to form another majority government."** (*Macleans*, Jan. 6/92)

But try as he might, Mulroney was unable to dispel the feelings Canadians held about him and his team. Even when things went right, Canadians were reminded why they felt the way they did.

When it comes to his children, Brian Mulroney seems to think the ABC's mean Anywhere But Canada.

How else to explain why the prime minister and his wife, Mila, opted to send their two eldest children to high-priced American schools?

Caroline, 19, is off to Harvard University to pursue an undergraduate degree.

Tuition at the Ivy League school is a mere $23,000 U.S. a year.

Son, Ben, 16, is attending Hotchkiss School in Lakeview, Conn., a prep school that has two gyms, 23 tennis courts, a swimming pool and 37 classrooms.

The cost: $15,500 U.S....

It's bad enough Mulroney signals he doesn't have confidence in our education system.

What's worse is he's affecting our children's future through federal cutbacks knowing full well that he can afford to get his kids an educational the best U.S. schools. (*Ottawa Sun*, Sept. 17/92)

By now the overwhelming majority of Canadians were convinced that what their Government said was not what it did. Once that conclusion had been reached, the end of the Mulroney administration was inevitable, though the members of his team hope that Canadians will forget their role in what took place and ask them for more of the same.

But will Canadians forget?

While campaigning for the leadership of the Conservative Party in March of 1983, Brian Mulroney said: **"we cannot practice exclusionary politics..."** (*Globe and Mail*, March 15/83). While campaigning for the leadership of the Conservative Party in March of 1993, Kim Campbell said she believed in **"the politics of inclusion"** (*Ottawa Citizen*, March 27/93).

After he won the leadership of the party, Mr. Mulroney promised **"to clean up once and for all"** the patronage system. He vowed his government would **"set up criteria for quality"** (Press Conference Transcript, July 9/84). After she won the leadership of the party, Ms. Campbell promised her government would create **"a list of desired qualifications and experience"** for patronage appointments. She vowed: **"I am declaring an immediate moratium on any new appointments..."** (Official Transcript, August. 9/93).

"Just a few hours after Prime Minister Kim Campbell gave a speech yesterday decrying patronage, the government announced that Biran Mulroney's former press secretary was Canada'a new ambassador to Cuba." (*Globe and Mail,* Aug. 10/93)

Kim Campbell served in Mulroney's inner cabinet, supports Mulroney's economic and constitutional policies, says Mulroney **"always comes down on the right side of an issue"**, sees in Canadians **"warmth"** and **"great respect"** for Mulroney, shares Mulroney's views about the **"enemies of Canada"**, and was, according to insiders, selected by Mulroney as his successor.

CONCLUSION

O' CANADA!

BRIAN MULRONEY SET OUT TO CHANGE the Conservative party. He wanted to give it a powerful Quebec wing. So he rounded up the remnants left by Maurice Duplessis' old *Union Nationale*, the party which gave Quebec the most corrupt government in the history of the country. To those remnants he added a bevy of quasi-separatists — some keen, some greedy.

True Conservatives simply don't know their party anymore.

Mulroney wanted to make international big business happy. And he did. He opened Canada for business, as he told them he would. He gave away access to Canada's natural resources. He helped them close down their Canadian branch plants and Canada's unique system controlling the price of patented drugs.

He set out to win the love and adulation of the Bay Street elite, but only succeeded for a while. He cut their taxes while increasing the taxes paid by the middle class. He forgot that big business wanted it all: low taxes and a reduced deficit at the expense of social programs.

He set out to make himself a big fellow with his cronies. And how they admired him for that! There were plenty of jobs, plums, and other nice things for the boys.

He set out to best Trudeau. Trudeau, he decided (on second thought) had failed; he would succeed. He rushed in where no angel would dare to tread, fanned dying embers, and thereby almost destroyed the country.

Mulroney set out to change politics in Canada. St. Laurent, Diefenbaker, Pearson, and Stanfield were old fuddy-duddies all! They actually believed in telling the truth. He did change politics in Canada, and came to be called "Lyin' Brian."

Many Canadians, though bitter and angry, are also embarassed and perhaps a bit sad to know that one of their Prime Ministers seems to have so richly earned such a nickname.

THE SHOW MUST NOT GO ON

And that's not just rhetoric. In fact, rhetoric about Mr. Mulroney and his team is superfluous because the record convicts more convincingly than any rhetoric could.

Mulroney set out to launch a new era in Canada and we now have the Record.

He and his team wanted to leave the legacy in safe hands.

They picked Kim Campbell.